Surviving Widowhood

Being reborn on the other side of grief

—a memoir

by

Eugene Campbell

Published by:
Eugene Campbell, Self-Publishing
P.O. Box 586
Palmer, MA 01069

Copyright © 1997 by Eugene Campbell
Original title: Memoirs of My Widowed Days

Cover design by Eugene Campbell
Author photo © Eugene Campbell

All rights reserved. No part of this book may be reproduced or transmitted in any form or by any means, electronic or mechanical, including photocopying, recording, or by information storage and retrieval system, without the written permission of the author, except where permitted by law.

Library of Congress Catalog Number: TXu 825-391
ISBN: 978-0-9793089-0-1

Manufactured in the United States of America

First printing, Van Volumes, LTD
2 Springfield Street
Three Rivers, MA 01080

March 2007

Contents

Preface	4
Disclaimer	5
Dedication	6
Acknowledgments	7
An Opening Word	9
Introduction	11

PART ONE – Our Life Before Her Death

Prologue 1	14
Chapter 1 – Our Early Years	15
Chapter 2 – Our Middle Years	39
Chapter 3 – Our Latter Years	44

PART TWO – Death Comes Between Us

Chapter 4 – A Few Months Before	51
Chapter 5 – The Date of Infamy	58
Chapter 6 – The First Few Months After	92

PART THREE – My Life in Solitude

Prologue 2	113
Chapter 7 – Reaching Out Against the Loneliness	115
Chapter 8 – Embracing Another Woman in My Life	137
Chapter 9 – Courting Again	155
Chapter 10 – The Recovery of My Consciousness	187
Chapter 11 – A New Awakening	205
Chapter 12 – Promises to Keep	229

PART FOUR – My Post Traumatic Life

Chapter 13 – Keeping My Vows	234
Chapter 14 – A New Direction For Living	242
Chapter 15 – Living Happily Ever After – Again	248

Postscript I	271
Epilogue	272
Postlude	274
The Author's Reflections	276
Postscript II	279
Recommended Reading	283

Preface

This memoir focuses on my experiences in dealing with the death of my wife. I write for the posterity of my immediate family and hopefully a wider audience comprised of widowers and widows. My story reveals in human terms the causes and events leading to my decision to stay single or marry again.

The book is divided into four parts, each comprising a significant portion of my life.

Surviving Widowhood

As a work of nonfiction

Disclaimer

In writing this memoir I have left the names of family and close friends intact, however, the names of the women I dated or courted or thought about dating and courting, have been changed to protect their identities and their lives. Not all of the women mentioned in this autobiography were actually courted. I have included some of my own personal thoughts and fantasies as narratives based on "What if?" situations with some women. These, "What if?" situations did not occur. These thoughts and fantasies however helped to form the reasons for decisions I made later.

To my wife Mary who resurrected the 21-year-old adult hidden deep inside of me for many years. She has developed and cultured a renewed faith in living and loving for both of us after the death of our spouses. It is by her encouragement this book has been written.

ACKNOWLEDGMENTS

My personal gratitude is extended to the following friends and family for their support and advice during my widowed days and their tolerance to my sorrow and inattentiveness while I recovered from my grief.

To Pastor Matthew Burt of the Evangelical Covenant Church of Springfield, Massachusetts for his good counsel and blessings and prayers, for conducting our wedding ceremony and the impact of his sermon on how woman was created to be a helpmate to man, that man cannot, nor should he, live alone.

To Barbara Wilson for starting her support group at the precise time I needed somewhere to go besides a singles bar or church; For providing that much needed meeting of the minds and place between alcohol and religion, and an open mind and open ear.

To Chaplain Everett Thompson for listening when I wasn't talking, for rendering help to a lost soul in a sea of depression and for conducting the service at my wife's funeral.

To the family members themselves, my daughters Tammy, Wendy and Melody, my son-in-laws Brian and Christopher and especially my grandchildren Heather and Richard whose being proves life and families do go on.

To the friends of the family, far too many to list individually, but when nearness counted they came and helped.

To my associates and fellow workers who tolerated my inattentiveness to work while I recovered from the loss of my wife.

To my publisher, Van Volumes, Russell Tate, making this book a reality.

December 2006
Massachusetts

Eugene Campbell

An Opening Word

I make this opening word to the women I met and on occasion dated or courted during my widowhood. Each of them, in her own way, has helped me return to the person I was before my late wife and I were married. It is from this person, not the person I was at the time of my wife's death that I have returned and elected to marry again instead of remaining single.

In my weaker moments I imagined how each and every one of them would have fared as a potential marital partner to me. There was little or nothing any of them did to promote or disqualify them selves from an auspicious partnership with me. It was through them however I discovered in myself what was best for me. A relationship between any of them and me would not have been completely sincere. They would have ended up living in my lie and to the standards of a deceased woman.

Even though I was closer to some women than others, the probability of a companionship could not exist. Therefore those relationships ended, in honesty, and remain, in friendship.

I take this opportunity to thank each of them, both knowingly and unknowingly, for what I have gained from our companies and to extend to them good luck and happiness for the rest of their lives. They each deserved a man better than me.

To those widowed men and women who haven't met another man or woman of your dreams yet I offer this advice; you will find whom you are seeking when you stop looking. I did.

INTRODUCTION

I found myself thrust into a life of being single again for three and a half years after Betty's death. I didn't say unexpected for I did expect her to precede me in death; I was not however fully prepared for the suddenness of it. Perhaps it was the complacency I developed over the years of waiting for what was inevitable that suppressed my expectation.

The first month following her death was more traumatic than I had prepared for. The mental and physical reality of being left alone in a couple world, surrounding myself with family and friends for a short period of time and then the ensuing solitude as each of them returned to their own lives and I resumed my own life being single again was disconcerting.

That month I called our families and friends living outside the state and asked for a gathering. We organized the funeral and the services together. Local friends organized the reception. As the day of the funeral ended I watched as each of them departed to return to their own lives and accepted their sympathies at my loss. Within a week, my own family from out of state went back to their lives. Except for one single daughter living at home, still attending school and an adopted mother, I was alone.

The first twelve months after the funeral brought me into contact with several other people who were single again and in despair, some were widowed, others had been divorced. A new singles group started shortly after Betty's death whose format contained just one rule; what you see here, what we say here, stays here. The group discussed, compared and shared their individual feelings, emotions and problems with each other. My narrative does not violate that condition. The issues and subjects we discussed in those meetings and how they influenced me is a part of my story. I have approached them as they impressed me, and me alone. These group discussions were a large part of my recovery in dealing with death and living single again.

A little more than a year after Betty's death I left the support group and went out on my own. During the group sessions and in the two years afterwards I tried, tested and cultivated what I had heard and learned through the group, my friends and family. I also read books on widowhood to ease my grief and romance books to learn what to look for in a companion. I encountered more failures than successes, but in a couple world you need succeed only once.

This then is my story about how I dealt with the trials, errors and tribulations of overcoming widowhood and how I managed to get back into life again as one half of a pair.

In sympathy to all who have walked this mile,

                                        Eugene Campbell

Prologue 1

October 19, 1992

The cradle of death holds the body of my departed wife. Her spirit has ascended leaving me alone and at great loss. Not just the body has been abandoned but my other consciousness as well, the essence of my successes and failures. From now on I must fend of myself and for myself. How do I do it? I know I can live alone, I also know I don't want to. But, where do I begin?

Chapter 1

Our Early Years

"See what happened when I wasn't looking."

A Chance Meeting

I had left the bus, lost and alone, that cool summer evening in July of 1963. I was looking forward to the three-day Independence Day weekend. Cold war events at work and off duty harassments in the squadron barracks had made life unbearable for me. The experienced drinkers I lived with kept laughing at me, the novice and I was becoming repulsed at their inane remarks during the last week. I made a conscious decision to go out drinking tonight and get myself plastered, if for no other reason than to experience another gut wrenching, head bursting drunk, but this time alone, for the second time since my 21st birthday a week before. Back then I had made a complete ass of myself in front of them.

    I asked some of the social type drinkers in the barracks where I could find a bar that few, if any, eager young women frequented. I was especially not in the mood for female companionship this night or to embarrass myself in the presence of the opposite gender. I got lots of advice and the name of one particular place, Hoff's Bar on East Colfax in Aurora. It seemed to fit the idea I had in mind. I put on my only dress suit and walked from the barracks out the north gate and down Yosemite Street to East Colfax Boulevard. I sat on the bench and naively waited for the next bus going east towards Fitzsimmons Army Hospital at the edge of the Aurora Township.

    Soon enough a bus stopped and I got on. I asked the driver to tell me when we got to the cross street nearest Hoff's Bar. He said, "Keep a sharp eye out for the sign on the right side. The bar is set back from the curb and won't be easy to see." I thanked him and took the nearest seat on that side of the bus.

    The drone of the diesel engine soon began to work on my tired mind. I stared semi-sightlessly into the night through the glared window, surrounded mostly by civilians, anxious to get home from work and a few more airmen like myself, excited over the prospect of leaving the base for the night.

The bus stopped every other block along Colfax. I had begun to think I might have missed my stop. I got up and asked the driver if we had. He said, "No. The bar is still a few blocks further down the road." I returned to my seat and to staring out the window.

I counted the bus stops in much the same manner as an insomniac would count sheep to relax. The bus stopped yet again. Still no bar was in sight. I yawned and stretched to regain my alertness. The bus pulled away from the curb and in the next block I spied the sign indicating Hoff's Bar outside my window. I pulled the cord to alert the driver to stop at the next corner as this seemed to be his routine.

He proceeded further down the street, first one block, then two, then three, then four and kept on going. I walked up the aisle. "Hey driver, I said, "we passed Hoff's Bar back there. Why won't you stop to let me off?" He replied, "The next bus stop is twelve blocks away. You'll have to wait until then to get off."

I became irate and disgusted with the driver as well as myself. I had specifically said the cross street nearest the bar not the next one after it. He could have told me to get off before passing the bar. I sat down near the door and waited for him to pull over and stop. I swear those twelve blocks seemed more like twelve miles by the time he finally let me off.

Under my breath I was swearing at him more than me for the long walk I'd have to make. After getting off the bus I turned up the collar of my suit against the cool night air and began walking back to the bar.

We had been advised and warned by our unit orderly rooms to be very careful when going out alone. Military towns were not renowned for their hospitality towards airmen. Every town had its share of troublemakers who would go out of their way to provoke an argument with a man in uniform. They needed no reason other than the knowledge the airmen couldn't or wouldn't fight back. We were easy to spot with our well-groomed haircuts and clean, pressed clothing. We were told; "Walk away - if you can."

I took hope that by being dressed in a black suit it would afford me some camouflage in the night. Walking back to the bar, I actually developed a fear of the streetlights and being readily visible to troublemakers or stalkers. Whenever possible I would walk closely behind another group of men and women acting like a straggler to their group. As each small group I followed stepped off into businesses, homes and apartments my fear of being assaulted was renewed.

Walking what I thought to be 12 blocks and still not having come upon the bar I began to look around for someone to give me directions. In another block I spotted a woman sitting under a tree in her front yard. The house was the third one up from the street, not too far away from Colfax if I needed to get back quickly. I decided to take a chance to approach her and ask for directions.

The shadows from the tree concealed her facial features. She was drinking from a highball glass. I approached her cautiously, not wanting her think I might be some kind of freak out to cause her harm.

Choosing to remain in the sidewalk, I called to her saying, "Excuse me miss, but could you tell me how much further it is to a place called Hoff's Bar?"

"Yes," she replied, "two blocks west."

Now, at my tender age of 21 years and being city born and bred, with little call for knowing east from we stand having learned only ten months ago my left foot from my right foot, I made the mistake of adding to my embarrassment by asking her to point in the correct direction. She pointed with her thumb over her shoulder towards the base. I thanked her and turned to leave.

She stopped me by asking; "You're new in town aren't you?"

"Not so new," I replied, "I've been here for months."

She inquired why I was dressed in a black suit and going to a saloon type bar. I became embarrassed and aware of my predicament. The revelation I had been duped by the troops in the barracks into wearing a formal suit to go to a western style bar didn't set too well with me. I coyly explained how my friends told me this was a bar of good culture and dignified people patronized it. She laughed at my gullibility. She was feeling frisky as was evidenced by the drink she was consuming, a mixed drink of some sort, I assumed. She asked me to sit and talk a spell. I thought it best not to, but she insisted. My strongest urge was to run like hell as fast as my feet could carry me and not stop at Hoff's Bar this time, either. On second thought, I felt if I did stay and talk a while she would eventually go back into the house and I could continue my plans to get drunk alone and unwind.

"Why are you sitting outside alone and drinking?" I asked her. She confided she had been in an argument with her in-laws and outlaws and had come outside for some fresh air and a quiet drink. Inside the house the air was stale, her friends very rowdy and the music too loud. She invited me to sit down on the grass with her. "The grass is wet and I'd prefer not to stain my suit." I told her.

"Wait here a moment while I get a blanket for you to sit on." She left the shadows of the tree for the front door.

In the dim light of the porch I made her out to be blonde, perhaps 21 or 22, a foot shorter than me and well figured. She was wearing a thin, nearly see-through white blouse and sawed off blue jeans that would barely pass for short shorts. On a different occasion I would find this meeting inviting. Tonight, however, I wasn't in the mood to socialize with women. My purpose for this evening was to find this particular bar and get drunk, alone. A female companion was not part of my plan. I mistakenly presumed she was as old as she looked.

She returned with a blanket and two fresh drinks offering one of them to me. I took it from her graciously, saying, "Thanks, but I really wasn't planning on staying long."

"Relax a while," she said, "the night is still young." She promoted more conversation by asking me the usual simplistic questions; what was my name, where was I born, where did I live before joining the Air Force, what did I study in school, how many brothers and sisters did I have and were both my parents still alive? I answered her questions courteously, without being totally revealing. Some of my answers were evasive. I felt no need to tell the absolute truth to a stranger. I think she picked up on that immediately. I asked her questions about the same subjects. Her answers were also polite, courteous and not totally revealing either. I felt as though we were playing a mind game of some sort with each other, each feeling out the other with some indeterminate goal in mind. I had no idea what it was and even less of an inkling of what it might bring.

A couple of drinks and much conversation later I reminded her it was getting late and I still had a bar I intended to go to. She laughed saying, "Do you really intend to go to a saloon type bar dressed like that?"

In my finest Scottish heritage I affirmed I was by saying, "Aye, I am!"

She said, "Excuse me, but this I've got to see! I think I'll tag along with you." By this time I felt comfortable with her so I consented to letting her join me.

We walked to Hoff's Bar by way of a short cut through a dark alley out of the bright lights of the boulevard.

When we got there I walked in like I had good sense coupled with the stubbornness of a common jackass. Two steps inside the door and a quick look around the bar and I wanted to finish my grand entry from under the welcome mat to the nearest, most dimly lit booth. Boy, did I feel stupid! I stood out all right, like a beacon on an aircraft-landing tower. I spotted my desire to right of the doorway and we went directly to it.

The girl, Betty was her name, restrained her laughter, took my hand and pulled me to the booth. I was dumb as well as stubborn. To me, not all lessons in life result in physical pain. The more important ones have their basis in mental anguish. I was certainly in that state.

A waitress appeared almost before we were seated. We ordered our drinks and listened in silence to the jukebox, which was playing "From a Jack to a Queen" by Ned Miller. Very quickly the waitress reappeared with our drinks. I paid for them and we resumed our topics of conversation from under the oak tree in greater detail.

I guzzled my beer. Betty sipped her ginger ale. We continued to talk and became less apprehensive of each other and any possible motives. Too soon it seemed the bartender announced last calls for drinks. The bar would close 30-minutes.

Just having turned the legal drinking age of 21 for the State of Colorado, the beer in the bar and the mixed drinks at her house made me real limber. Betty's easygoing nature, I felt, was directed more at my condition than her sodas. They made her giddy, as I would learn more about later. We finished our last drink and I offered to walk her home.

Back at the house we sat on the front porch and continued talking. Somewhere in time one of her relatives ventured out of the house to see find out where she'd been and what she had been doing. She explained to him briefly the events of the last two hours. The gentleman introduced himself and by those introductions we discovered we were all associated with the military in some form or another, active duty, retired, spouse or dependent child. Betty was the only true civilian and, I was informed - a minor. The revelation floored me! Contributing to the delinquency of a minor! Oh shit! I stared at her and she simply smiled back. Oh my God, what have I done? I thought hard, real hard, as hard as the alcohol would allow me. Did I ever ask her age? No. I sure didn't. I assumed she was as old as she looked. I contained my fear and anger by laughing at my own stupidity.

I was invited by her relatives to stay the night. I accepted because it was well after midnight. The north gate on Yosemite would be closed at this late hour. The main gate on 6th Avenue stayed open for 24 hours but that would be an extra two miles to walk. Also, the buses had stopped running at midnight. We continued to talk. Around 3:00 am I fell asleep on the couch. Booze, the humid air in the house and Betty's voice had begun to sound more like rambling had burdened my fatigue. She spent the night on the love seat opposite me.

In the morning a lady came in, another Betty as I learned later, found us together in the living room and went into shock and became angry. She had conjured up a picture of illicit love making between us during the night. It took some intense talking by "Baby" Betty but she was finally convinced there had not been any "hanky panky" as she put it. As I came to understand the situation the older Betty was babysitting the younger Betty for the weekend.

Soon the rest of the household began to resurrect itself and the older Betty began to make breakfast for everyone. I was hung over. My head hurt real badly but I was able to make the faces and names come together.

I was invited to stay for breakfast and join with the families and their holiday weekend activities. I accepted the free breakfast but declined the remaining invitation. I was still feeling sheepish, not guilty, at staying overnight and then being accused of having sex relations with a minor.

After breakfast and a pot of coffee I said good-bye and thanked everyone for their hospitalities. I was invited to return anytime. I half promised to come back the next weekend if I wasn't on duty. Betty gave me her phone number. I said I might take her up on the invitation provided her parents agreed.

The following weekend I was free and decided to see Betty again. I called the number she gave me and spoke to her. She had already received her mother's permission to go to the modified stock car races with me on Sunday, with one proviso; I had to meet the family. "Okay," I said. It was a small price to pay. She gave me the directions on how to find the apartment her parents lived in.

The bus ride into downtown Denver was long and boring: the bus stopping every other block for passengers. There were no 12-block spaces in this direction. The ride took 45 minutes to the cross street I was to get off at. From there it took another 10 minutes to locate the apartment building where she lived. That left me with five minutes to find the apartment. I arrived at their door precisely on time. I met her mother and stepfather. Her mother was an Amazon of a woman and her stepfather a dwarf by comparison. Both were very kind and very polite. We visited for half an hour then Betty announced we had to leave to catch a bus to the racetrack.

The ride to Lakewood lasted an hour. The racetrack was adjacent to an amusement park. We had to walk through it to get to the track. Betty hadn't mentioned that particular detail. My own thoughts were that the amusement park would have been more inviting. I asked about taking in some fun and games for a while. She explained she was not the fun and games type where this amusement park was concerned but perhaps another time. Our date tonight evidently had a singular purpose.

At the racetrack she went all the way to the top of the bleachers and sat down to wait for the time trials to begin. As we sat there drivers brought out their cars for warm up laps and testing after making adjustments in the pits.

In between the deafening roars of the warm up laps I asked her more questions about her and her family. In summary it went like this. She had moved to Denver with her mother and sister from Ohio shortly after her father died at age 43. He was a blue baby at birth. In declining health he needed surgery to correct his heart ailment. Although the surgery went well he succumbed to complications involving pneumonia. Her mother sold the estate and moved to Denver to be nearer her own relatives. Her mother had remarried recently and the four of them, which included a younger sister, were living together in the two-bedroom apartment. The arrangement wasn't the best set of circumstances. Still, it wasn't all that bad.

The time trials started and that ended our casual conversation. We stayed to watch all the races. I knew my ears would still be roaring in the morning. We got back to downtown Denver 10 minutes before the last bus to Aurora came by. She bid me good night at the corner. I was hesitant to leave her there, alone and so far from home, but she insisted I leave. If I walked her home I'd miss the last bus. It would take me until sunrise to walk back to the base from her place. There would be no guarantee I could make the morning formation and roll call. I reluctantly conceded to her reasoning and left her at the corner. I got back to the base and the barracks by 1:00 am. I managed to get in four hours sleep before getting up and going to work.

Our courtship lasted three months. In that time I proposed three times, on August 4th, September 4thand lastly on October 4th. That day I presented myself at her parent's apartment door and stated, "Today is the day." I was in love enough to get married. We were friends enough to let that love grow. We'd spent $870.00 courting. I had $30.00 left by which to get married or cease seeing one another. She thought I was crazy, which I was, but she went along with my petty charade as she called it. To her, my desire to get married was a joke. Her mother took her aside and talked to her privately. (I learned later she and her mother were discussing the merits of a marriage license over a driver's license. Betty was holding out for the driver's license.) After much secluded conversation and debate her mother convinced her she could always get a driver's license, marriage proposals weren't that common. Her mother felt I was sincere and the other members of the family, aunts, uncles, cousins and a few select friends I'd met over the last three months thought I would be a great catch and she should go for it. Betty finally relented and agreed to go along with this marriage idea for as far as I would go with it. Well, she still thought it was an elaborate joke up until the time we entered the judge's chambers. It wasn't until then and only then, did she realize we were actually getting married. The real laugh was indeed on her. We were married October 4, 1963 at 3:50 pm. Her mother and the judge's secretary witnessed the ceremony.

When I recovered from my elated state on the bus ride to our apartment I discovered I had forgotten to pay the judge. Betty suggested we start our marriage with a finer dinner instead. He didn't really require payment for his services. As a federal judge it was part of his normal duties. I finally relented and we went shopping for a meal fit for a king and his queen.

Our wedding night meal consisted of two very large T-bone steaks, baked potatoes, canned corn and for a wedding cake - two Hostess Cupcakes with a candle in each, a hefty trip to the grocery store in those times. After buying the license, the wedding rings, paying for the laboratory tests and dinner, I had a $1.59 left in my pocket. My next payday was ten days away. What a way to start a marriage.

Within six months of our wedding the Titan I missile system I worked on was deactivated and we were transferred to Little Rock AFB in Arkansas where I was to work on the newer Titan II. Little did we realize what events would take place there that would contribute to her death.

A Medical Miscalculation

Our feature social event in Little Rock was playing pinochle with friends and neighbors at the base recreation club. It was during one of the tournament contests Betty complained her left leg felt cold. I touched it and it was indeed cold, very cold. She said she could stand okay and walk on it but the cold sensation remained. We decided to leave the tournament and go to the hospital.

After some examinations and tests she was admitted. A massive blood clot in the groin of her left leg had cut off all circulation to her leg. I asked (nearly pleaded) about surgically removing it but the doctor explained that current administrative protocols dictated nonsurgical means as the first course of action. This doctrine was initiated after numerous reports of excessive and unwarranted operations were being performed in hospitals. I developed a grave feeling in the pit of my stomach over this doctrine. I felt it was a knee jerk reaction towards all surgeries and not just those being abused. His alternative solution was to use chemical therapy to dissolve the clot that had been caused by the birth control pills she was taking to regulate her cycle. (It would be another 15 years before science discovered this particular birth control pill caused clotting among her blood type.) The clot was successfully broken up chemically. The negative side effect however, was one large clot became 18 smaller clots, which lodged themselves in the smaller veins below the knee. This "alternate solution" caused her much pain and suffering until her death. In later years, several specialists would recommend the surgical stripping of those veins as the better alternative to her continued suffering. Surgery however was still a dirty word, even in those days. She was treated for months with alternate doses of Vitamin "K" and Coummadin in an effort to stabilize her condition. Her blood proved too reactive to accomplish this stability.

It took about seven years from the day of the initial clot, to arrive at a point where nothing else could be done, or was advisable. Her condition had stabilized somewhat in that wearing surgical hosiery helped to alleviate the pain created when her leg would swell up for a few minutes then contract back to normal size. It seemed to have a lung of its own.

During this seven-year period she started bowling as an exercise. From the best medical judgment this sport should have proven harmful to her condition, but, as it turned out, bowling actually helped to set the clots in place. Before bowling I would wrap her leg very snuggly with an Ace type bandage. Her leg would swell but the pressure was maintained on the clots helping to keep them in place. After bowling, she would elevate her leg and I would remove the bandage. The swelling would subside and she would be fine.

The condition of her leg decided for me to make the military a career. I could never afford the cost of her medical care in a civilian sector lifestyle. The Air Force had the responsibility for her health care for life by having created the condition that she must live with and more likely die by.

At our last visit with a specialist I was told by the doctor a day could come when I might wake up in bed with a dead wife beside me and I should begin preparing myself for that eventuality. That, of course, was my worse case scenario. She could die while not in bed at all. To make matters worse, he confided to me that there was every possibility a clot could move at any time, lodge in the lung or heart and that it would be her end. Even if such an event occurred in a hospital, or on an operating table, the chances for her survival were close to nothing. Additionally he did not recommend pregnancy. The complications could also prove deadly.

Armed and alarmed with this information I spent our remaining years together sleeping with one hand on her body.

Shortly after the doctor's revelation I decided to change specialties. The missile field took me away from home nearly daily and for long distances. I felt it best to remain as close to her as I could without wearing the same pair of shoes. I talked to a career counselor at base personnel and he recommended a carpentry career as a change. I took his advice.

My idea and decision was practical enough, however, I didn't count on becoming available for overseas duty by changing careers. In the missile field I was stateside bound. In my new job as a carpenter, I became eligible for worldwide assignments. To my great dismay my name came up for Southeast Asia during the Vietnam Conflict. To make matters worse, Betty became pregnant three months before shipping out. The best laid plans of mice and men are easily thwarted by war.

The Latent Affects and How They Were Dealt With

I went to the Vietnam War zone in March 1967 and sent Betty to Ohio to live with her grandparents until I returned. It was a great event for her. She could give birth to the first great-grandchild and be living with the great-grand parents too. I, on the other hand, would be half a world away. Should anything go wrong, I wouldn't be back for 24 hours and a dateline crossing.

In mid-July I received a Red Cross message late in the afternoon. After skipping one line the remaining message was typed over itself making the message senseless and impossible to read. All we knew was a problem existed. The nature and extent was unknown. The Red Cross director informed me he had already requested a retransmitted message. There was nothing I could do but wait. He couldn't make any arrangements for an emergency trip home without a clear message stating the problem. He did suggest that a Military Affiliate Radio Station (MARS) call might give me some peace of mind. I took him up on his suggestion. He contacted the MARS Office and made the arrangements.

    The call was placed at minus 14 hours GMT. It would be 6:00 pm in the evening in Ohio. I talked to Betty's aunt. The baby was fine, a girl. She was classed premature by being two ounces underweight and hadn't been to sleep since being born. Betty was okay through the delivery, but while she was in the recovery room a blood clot moved and lodged in her lung. The doctors were still consulting on what to do. I told Aunt Vee I needed to see for myself what her actual condition was. I needed to come home. I explained what happened to the first message. She said she'd talk to her father and have him contact the Red Cross again.

    It took a full 24 hours to get a proper message through. I had packed my bags and stored the rest of my stuff in my footlocker in anticipation. With a legible message in my hands and a set of emergency orders, I was going home.

The next available flight took the nickel tour of the Pacific Ocean and Alaska. 28½ hours of flying around a Pacific Depression. The bummer was, the plane that departed Bangkok four hours after mine went straight back to San Francisco - nonstop, a trip of 18 hours without a tailwind. Double the bummer, I encountered a two-hour layover in the San Francisco Bay area by missing earlier flights. Next was the Red Eye to Cleveland and a connecting flight to Youngstown. Grandpa met me at the airport. He told me Grandma and Aunt Vee were at home tending to the baby. Betty was still at the hospital. He gave me the option of where to go. Since the baby was being taken care of, I opted to go to the hospital.

When I saw Betty she was sitting up in bed smoking. I asked her if this wasn't counter-productive. "No," she replied, "doctor's orders." The "cigarette" was a medicinal type. She had to smoke it to make her cough. These cigarettes and the coughing they induced, would force the blood clot out orally. Two days later it did. Another 24 hours of testing and observation and she was released.

We spent one week in turmoil and three weeks in bliss with an impromptu 30-day leave and a newborn baby.

I returned to Southeast Asia exactly 30 days later. Since this trip was of an emergency nature the leave was not added to my tour. I went to see the Red Cross director the morning after I returned. He was noticeably disturbed with me. His primary concern was why had I come back? I simply stated, "Both the baby and the mother survived, why not?" He explained in cases like mine it was customary to apply for a transfer and have the tour of duty curtailed for one year and he had expected me to apply for an emergency transfer. I understood his reasoning but not his concern. If I had exercised that option I would have been sent back in 12 months; Randolph Personnel Center would have seen to that. If either the baby or the mother had died I would have applied for a transfer or discharge. However, in light of the events, I decided to return and complete the tour of duty. Another point I kept reserved in the back of my mind was that Southeast Asia returnees received consecutive overseas tours or base of preference assignments stateside upon completion of their tours. I would have blown an exceptional opportunity to get to go to England, which was my hearts desire if I did not complete my tour. This he did not need to know.

When rotation time came up I got my first base of choice - stateside, a return assignment to Lowry AFB in Denver. On the surface this seemed an exceptional assignment, however, in retrospect, maybe not so good for me.

I had left Lowry AFB as a missile man; I would be returning as a carpenter. Lowry was an older World War II base in the Air Force inventory with too many wooden structures long past their life expectancies.

Well, at least Betty would be back close to her family and Denver was a good assignment as civilian and country living goes. I gambled and lost out on an exceptional opportunity of going to England.

I was 30 days from returning stateside when the First Sergeant called me into his office to say there was a priority change in my next assignment and I was to report to the base personnel office immediately. Not knowing what could make or cause a priority change in my assignment I dropped my hammer and left for base headquarters. At the assignment section I read the assignment change: I was being sent to England after all! Hallelujah! The priority in the assignment change was for Betty and our daughter to get passports and for the household goods to be returned from Denver, unloaded and repacked for overseas shipment. This would be a nice trick to accomplish in 30 days. Oh well, it would be up to her to get it all done. I couldn't help except to send her the necessary paperwork.

Much to my surprise the movers did return the household goods, they were repacked for overseas shipment and she did get her and the baby's passport - all in less than 30 days.

We spent ten days short of five years in England. Betty gave birth to two stillborn sons and one live daughter during the tour. Her blood clots continued to cause problems and concerns. Three more blood clots moved. Both passed through the heart and lungs without creating or causing a serious problem. Out of the 18 blood clots four had moved thus far. It was frightening to think when the next 14 might move and what might happen. Our next assignment took us to Vandenberg AFB and the second best tour of duty we would enjoy in my career. We made some conscientious decisions to improve the odds with the blood clots and pregnancies.

Chapter 2

Our Middle Years

"Living in fear with Death's hand on the doorknob."

Development of Those Initial Fears

Our tour of Vandenberg didn't last long. It was ended by my promotion. Being promoted made me excess to the base needs based on quotas versus allocations to authorized slots. While at Vandenberg AFB Betty gave birth again, this time another daughter. But I'm getting ahead of myself.

En route to Vandenberg AFB Betty conceived again. The event was made more difficult by being on the road. The pregnancy didn't last long; she aborted in the second month. The attending obstetrician recommended we stop trying so hard for a family. We had two healthy happy daughters and the doctor said we were playing a dangerous game of Russian roulette with her body. The physical changes that took place during pregnancies were jeopardizing her life and he felt, unnecessarily. His recommendation was to consult with the Ob/Gyn clinic at our next base and look into sterilization very seriously. Actually we weren't really trying as hard for a family as he thought. By calculation, Betty conceived every six weeks from the date of our marriage and following a miscarriage or a birth up until she was sterilized.

The issue of sterilization was not easy to solve nor was the decision to proceed and how and to whom. At the time California law imposed many restrictions on such a procedure. In part the ages of the couple and the number of children currently at home were significant points. The state's "golden numbers" were both parents over 30 years of age and three children already living at home. Betty was four years from being 30 and we only had two kids. The law barely made allowances for physical conditions. They had to be extreme.

It took three months of discussions and haggling but we finally convinced the base doctors and satisfied the State of California our case was extreme and unusual. We decided Betty would be sterilized instead of me. The decision was a conscientious one. She had the blood clot problem, it was her health at risk, not mine. If I were to die suddenly or unexpectedly and she remarried and became pregnant again, then died as a result of a blood clot moving, our children would be left alone without even one natural parent. The odds were slim but better than a blood clot moving.

Betty was scheduled for a new type of treatment, a TL Scope surgery. In simple terms, the stomach is inflated, a scope and probe are inserted into the abdomen through the naval and the tubes are seared apart electronically. The odds of another pregnancy are zero. She would have to undergo pregnancy testing 24 hours prior to surgery. If the test were negative the surgery would be performed the following morning.

My next plan should have been a week's vacation - alone. The pregnancy test came back positive - Somewhere in the vicinity of 24-72 hours of conception. Our third child was another daughter. There were no complications during the pregnancy however; a check of her blood clots disclosed another to be missing. Five deliveries, five blood clots moved. The coincidences weren't too encouraging.

Betty had been scheduled for sterilization following the birth of our 3rd daughter. Although delayed, the surgery was accomplished. We were compelled to wait another six weeks after the birth of our daughter because the doctor didn't arrive in time for the delivery to perform the TL Scope procedure immediately after birth.

Getting On With Living

We felt we finally had some assurances of safety from blood clots at last. I point out in retrospect that during our marriage we produced a horrible score card as child bearing goes. Betty conceived 18 times, 10 males and 8 females. Of the 18 conceptions she delivered 3 live births, all girls, 2 stillborns, both boys and miscarried 10 boys and 3 girls at various stages of pregnancy between six weeks and six months. Needless to say it was a horrendous period in our lives. Fetal and child losses aside, the constant concerns over her dying by a blood clot moving certainly made our early years of marriage nerve wracking.

With the arrival of our last child, change of station orders came again. This time we were going overseas.

In the next seven years we lived as a family in the Philippines, she and the girls lived in Oregon while I was stationed in Alaska, as a family again in Texas and North Dakota. Then finally, we returned to the Vandenberg area in retirement.

During this time we began to rest easier, for the fears of her dying from a blood clot diminished. Her condition had stabilized for the most part. There were the usual and accepted pains in her leg brought on by prolonged standing and walking, but nothing further regarding her blood clots and their moving after a pregnancy. We felt safe and assured our decisions at Vandenberg AFB worked and were correct. Betty's condition seemed to have stabilized. The time bomb was still ticking however, only now it was ticking silently.

Chapter 3

Our Latter Years

"Complacency is not a place to visit."

How Time and Circumstances Erased the Fears and Events Leading to Complacency

My last assignment in North Dakota turned sour in two years. I had in that time attained the prestigious predicament of completing 20 years of military service. Being in that enviable position and foreseeing my military career coming to an inevitable end, I elected to retire and submitted my request. We returned to the Vandenberg AFB area before Christmas. The job I had hoped to get in a bowling center never materialized. We were left broke and penniless for nearly two months. College classes started in January and I began drawing tuition assistance through the V.A. It helped keep the wolf away from the door.

After nine months of unemployment I finally got a job in a small manufacturing firm in a nearby township. The drive there and back ate up half of my paycheck. It wasn't financial security, but it put an end to humiliating food stamp assistance.

Three months later I got a job offer from civil service and an appointment opportunity. I was selected and took the position. The pay was triple what I was making and the drive to work was only one third the distance.

We stayed in the Vandenberg area for 6½ years. Slowly, the inflation in California began to catch up with our income. Staying for seven years and beyond meant bankruptcy. With all other options and alternatives exhausted we were left with selling out and moving. We transferred to Idaho.

Our decision to relocate was prompted and motivated by a family reunion. I knew we were approaching bankruptcy and I was looking for alternate ways to avoid it. Selling the house and moving wasn't our primary choice. We were happy in Lompoc and the social aspects of life in the community and the friends we had made, but economics is a powerful issue. I wasn't having any luck coming up with answers. It was during this time of depression we received an invitation to attend a 25th annual family reunion in Colorado. My computations indicated it would cost us every cent we had in savings to make the trip. With burden in my heart I threw caution to the wind and agreed to go.

The trip took two days from Lompoc to Saint George and to Denver. We spent the second night in Denver with Betty's relatives. The cousins, all girls, had never seen one another in the 25 years since the parents met each other and married. Of all the cousins in the group, Betty was the only one to have remained married since 1963. Her other cousins had married twice.

The next generation of cousins was up well into the night getting acquainted. The following morning we headed for Lake McConaughy in Ogallala, Nebraska. We would meet the rest of the families at the lake.

Our trip there took six hours. It was a great occasion. Our family spent a total of eight days on the lake, fishing (a first priority), visiting, camping, movies and a family party that doubled as a birthday celebration. Several pictures were taken. One picture in particular, that I took, would prove to be heartbreaking later. Six members of the family posed for the photo, five cousins and an uncle. Within the next six years, three of the members, every other person in the photo, would be dead. Betty was one of the people in the photo. It is a difficult picture to look at even to this day.

My leisure time was spent talking to the local folks. I wondered how they managed to live here and at what cost? One fellow I talked to had retired from his job in Florida, sold his house, came to Nebraska, bought and paid cash for his home here and raised a small herd of cattle which he sold every year. The incomes from his retirement, the sale of his house and the cattle kept him comfortable and occupied, not busy. Another fellow I talked to simply sold out and moved. The cost of a prefabricated home on the lake was reasonable and left him with a fair savings account similar to an IRA. He spent most of his days hunting and fishing and doing odd jobs for pocket money. There were many more similar stories but these two helped to formulate a plan in my mind.

Those stories gave me new hopes to pursue when we returned to California. I was still opposed to selling out and moving. I preferred a transfer to another job within the federal service system if possible so we might return to our home when our economic situation stabilized. Where and how it might work was another matter. Our health conditions would also dictate. I began to feel selling out might not be as gloomy as I anticipated.

Betty had an acquired condition in her feet. They looked and felt like a riverbed, dry and brittle. Within a week of walking in the sand surrounding the lake her soles were healed. For the first time since I could remember, 25 years, they were soft and moist. For myself, my breathing had improved slightly. I was less dependent on inhalers. The trip as a reunion was taking on added blessings I had not thought possible.

When the vacation was over and we started back, Betty looked at me intently. The distant look in my face meant I was considering moving. She wasn't especially happy. I was looking beyond bankruptcy and into improved health for both of us. Our children were flexible. They had spent their whole lives in and around the military and were quite used to packing and moving. For them it was a normal event.

I didn't jump headlong into selling out and moving. I kept the idea in reserve but not as remotely. My first concern was improving the cash flow and avoiding bankruptcy at all costs. I also looked intently into transfers to other bases in other states as well as other jobs including overseas assignments to avoid losing the house. I spent the better part of the next four months in my quest.

Jobs overseas were scarce in my series and my other qualifications. The prospects and choices were likewise limited. An overseas transfer would at least allow us to keep the house we had waited and worked so long to have. When the overseas job possibility was eliminated I resigned myself to the fact selling out and moving was our sole option. Eventually, I settled for a career registry, signed up and sat back to wait. In less than three weeks I had three offers pending, two in Idaho and one in Colorado. I decided to accept the first one to select me. It was the Idaho offer that came first.

Within another four weeks I had orders and a new job in a new series - Housing Management. I left the family behind and reported to my new position. I spent eight weeks in Idaho breaking into the new job, going to school and finding a house. Returning to Lompoc, we sold our home, watched our second daughter graduate from high school and returned to Idaho bag and baggage. The year was 1989. The first of the three people in the photo I took had already died, her younger cousin, of pneumonia. In three years the next person in the photo would be dead - Betty. Her uncle would die the following year.

Along the Road

I walked a mile with Pleasure,

She chatted all the way,

But left me none the wiser

For all she had to say.

I walked a mile with Sorrow,

And ne'er a word said she,

But, oh, the things I learned from her

When Sorrow walked with me!

— Robert Browning Hamilton

Chapter 4

A Few Months Before

"Happiness in being grandparents."

Euphoria and Pain

We were the proud grandparents of a granddaughter in June 1992 and a grandson in October 1992. The trip to Victorville in June was the first of both auspicious occasions. For Betty both were touched by misery.

Foot Trouble and Surgery

Two months before our first trip X-rays detected an "extra" bone in her right foot. It had been there since birth but only recently shifted from its secluded position to a point where it had become visible to doctors. With medication to ease the pain and restrictive activities she was able to get around until surgery was performed early in June.

Our daughter Melody was scheduled for foot surgery on the same morning to alleviate a bunion condition. Melody went in first, followed by her mother. (I would have two weeks of nursing two incapacitated females. Not a very inspiring thought.) Both surgeries went well. And there were no complications with the blood clots for Betty.

Melody started school three months after surgery. Betty on the other hand wasn't healing painlessly. Even with prosthesis and restrictive activities she continued to suffer. Our plans for going to the old mining town of Silver City for our 29th wedding anniversary were cancelled due to it. Adding complications to the occasion, our daughter Wendy was expecting and due around our anniversary date.

Heather

We were still asleep in bed on Father's Day when the phone rang. Betty answered it. Brian called to say, "It's a girl!" Betty listened to the details intently. Heather was premature by weight, the same as her mother years ago, but should be able to come home in three days.

I had greased the wheels for a leave of absence with my supervisor before leaving work on Friday that in the event of the birth of our first grandchild over the weekend I could take an impromptu leave of absence. I contacted him later in the morning to confirm the blessed event and let him know we'd be leaving for Victorville Monday morning. He was pleased and happy for the new parents and us.

We left home around 7:00 am Monday morning. Betty wasn't able so I had to drive the whole distance there and back. The trip across the deserts of Idaho, Nevada and California leave a lot to be desired, namely scenery. It was boring and not without suffering, mine mostly. Betty was sedate in her relaxed passenger position by not having to apply pedal pressure to her right foot. I, on the other hand, felt like I was developing bedsores seated in a fixed position for over 900 miles. Except for gas, food and toilet breaks I had little or no relief from the motionlessness. I was grateful for our arrival in Victorville.

I went up the stairs to the apartment as if I were 25 years old again. Betty was as slow as the proverbial slug. I was already holding Heather when she got to the door. She was very tiny. We were surprised to find both mother and daughter home so soon after birth. The short of the story was - if no complications following birth were encountered then medical insurance no longer covered stays over 24 hours. Heather's birth weight was not a major concern so she was sent home with her mother the next day.

I observed Betty was reluctant to hold Heather initially. I didn't question her hesitance at the time. I thought it better to keep the incident to myself until later, when we were on our way home. We stayed for four days. Betty was a chatterbox all the way home alleviating some of my boredom from another desert crossing. I forgot completely to question her about her hesitance to hold Heather until after our grandson was born.

Richard

Betty called me at work on Friday afternoon to say, "It's a boy this time!" I went to inform my supervisor. He suggested I go on an extended inspection visit for the rest of the day. I agreed. My mind certainly wouldn't be on work and if I stayed and I'd be a safety hazard to everyone around me. I drove home in a bit of a daze.

Finally, a male offspring! What grandiose thoughts I had! A granddaughter and a grandson in one year! I could work freely on toys and other things like any grandfather who could, would. Not all one gender. Betty should be walking on cloud nine. How long had we hoped for at least one child of each sex, for ourselves or for our children, a boy and a namesake at that, Richard Michael, the given middle names of both his maternal grandfather and father.

The truck rumbled and shook. "What the hell was that?" I asked myself aloud. Oh crap, the railroad tracks already. I must have been day dreaming more intently than usual. "Arrive alive you dummy!" I said aloud to myself, "or you won't live to see your grandson!"

When I arrived at home Betty was talking to her adopted mother Betty about the happy event and arranging for her to start house sitting. I assembled a list of my concerns and briefed her orally on each item.

Then I left them to continue their discussion and started packing. Betty came in to help me and told me Wendy had had a rough time but was doing well. During the delivery her kidneys had shut down but the doctor got them restarted. Chris had been very worried.

The next morning we left a half hour later than planned. "Not to worry," I assured her, "we can still arrive by 11:00 PM at the latest. "We have enough safety factored in." Betty was a chatterbox all the way to San Francisco. Another grandchild.

We arrived at 10:30 pm, an hour later than I planned but within the "no later than" arrival time of 11:00 pm. Chris said we could go right to the hospital to see Wendy and Richard. He had made plans for a late visit. We stayed with Wendy and Richard for an hour and left. Wendy looked real rough. She was aware of our presence but was still at the edge of never-never land. We went home to unload and unpack.

Chris' father David had arrived the day before us and had returned to the house while we were at the hospital. I unloaded our car and the cradle I built for their children to use and assembled it. I showed Chris how to put it together and how to store it. He was pleased and David was impressed.

David had bought an expandable crib, bed and dressing table modular unit for Richard. I was impressed also.

Wendy and Richard came home on Tuesday. We stayed through Wednesday. We left on Thursday, driving all day to make it back home by midnight.

During the trip back Betty was pleased as punch. I had never seen her so happy. She was particularly pleased because there was a (grand) son of sorts to carry on the family line, not the name, just the line. I suppose in a paternal society women will maintain the name thing is only a legal point of view, not biological, whereas men see more tangible results in the name thing.

But I was mostly interested in why she exhibited so much more enthusiasm as a grandmother with Richard than with Heather, the question being reborn from the trip to Victorville and my forgetfulness. I asked her and her response was, "Heather was more delicate."

"True," I stated, "but no more so than her mother Tammy."

"That was also true," she said and added, "but when Tammy was born she was confined to an incubator and I had held her only briefly. The bonding process was incomplete, unfulfilling." Betty confessed she had been a little bit terrified of a baby so tiny. Richard on the other hand was quite huge. At any rate, there was logic and understanding from my observations. She wasn't unhappy with Heather quite the reverse, only fearful of her size.

We arrived home just before 11:00 pm, beat, bushed and battered from another desert crossing and meeting old man winter coming back. A broken snow floor is not a peaceful country drive. We crashed into bed very soon after unloading the car and showing the pictures of our recent events to our house sitter.

The following morning we regrouped and started putting everything away. Friday was bingo night at the Memorial Hall and we were part of the work crew. Bingo went well. We returned home about 10:30 pm, still suffering a little from jet lag but feeling better.

Chapter 5

The Day of Infamy

"Death brings more family and friends together than life."

The Events That Occurred the Day Betty Died and Through the Memorial Service

We stayed up until half past midnight. I had developed some gas after my before-bed-time snack. I took some medication and rested in an inclined position. Betty told me she was going to have a cigarette and read some more. I said, "Fine, if I roll over and go to sleep after this belly ache subsides, cuddle up." I must have drifted off to sleep very shortly afterwards, similar to have calling my anesthesiologist "My friend Ken," just before my gall bladder surgery. Fatigue, past events and relief from the gas pains finally caught up to me.

    I awoke with a jump-start at 2:52 am according to the clock on the headboard. I heard snoring, heavy snoring and the thought came to me, I'm the only one who snores in this household. Had Betty started? I rolled over to see if it was her but she wasn't in bed. The bed was wet on her side. I tried to clear my head. Something was wrong but I was still caught in the throes of deep slumber. Slowly my head began to become more conscious. The snoring was coming from the bathroom. I called out, "Betty. Betty?" She didn't reply. I rolled back to my side of the bed and got up. My legs were wobbling more than if I was getting up to use the toilet. I stumbled around the end of the bed and the blanket box. I normally made this trip with my eyes closed, much as a blind person would, but on this occasion, with my eyes open, I couldn't manage the trodden path without walking into the furniture.

    I saw a pair of feet lying on the floor in the bathroom as I began to get around the blanket box. I wasn't sure of what I was looking at or who but Betty was the only one I was looking for. I called out again, "Betty. Betty!" Still no reply. The snoring was definitely coming from the bathroom. Lying on the floor in the moonlight was Betty.

She was lying on her right side with her right arm behind her. She was snoring! I called to her, "Betty. Betty! Betty!!" Still no reply. Why in the world is she laying on the floor I asked myself? Did she fall asleep? No, not likely. She doesn't look as if she fell off the toilet either. The position she's lying in is wrong.

Did she trip and fall? I looked closer and harder. Damn, this isn't right I told myself. Something is seriously wrong! I knelt down beside her as best as I could. Our bathroom might be larger than any other we had in any home we lived in before but it was narrow. Two people couldn't pass one another in opposite directions.

I was becoming more awake now. The adrenaline was kicking in and working overtime. As I knelt closer I noticed blood around her nose and mouth. It wasn't running. It was just there. There wasn't a pool of blood on the carpet, hardly a trace, a few spots at most. Terror began to fill my soul! I called to her again, "Betty? Betty. Betty! Answer me! Dear God I thought, this can't be happening, this can't be real. No, not this, not now! I need help! Betty needs help!

I tried to roll Betty over but her arm behind her back prevented me from doing so. "Shit!" I muttered. I called to her again, "Betty!" Still no response. What to do? Call for help. Get to the phone and hurry! My heart was beginning to pound like a runaway air powered hammer. I stood and backed up towards the bathroom entry door. Clear of her body I turned towards the door to our bedroom.

I hurried to the phone. *What's the number for emergencies*? I thought to myself. I couldn't remember! I shook my head and then it came to me! I pressed 911; I don't know how I managed to dial in the moonlight. I didn't have the cognitive sense to turn on the lights. I felt a cold wet spot where I put my knee on the bed. A voice answered, "Emergency Services, how can I help you?" I told the feminine voice my wife was laying on the bathroom floor with blood around her nose and mouth and won't respond to her name or my speaking to her. The operator asked if she was still breathing, the EMT's had to know. I said, "Yes, I believe so. She's making a snoring sound."

"What is your address?" she asked? I told her. "I'll notify the EMT's right away."

I went back to look at Betty again. She was still the same. I went to the dresser and pulled on a pair of sweat pants. Then I went to the side door to let the EMT's in.

A police car arrived first. It pulled up into the driveway and then it stopped and backed out again, appearing to be leaving. I went out the door and saw the officer park in front of the house at the curb and start walking up the sidewalk to the front door. *Oh shit*, I thought, *I've got to go back into the house, through the hallway, to the front door and unlock it for the officer.* I made it just as he knocked. I took him to the bathroom. He asked how long Betty had been lying there. I told him I didn't know. I found her on the floor at 2:52 am on my bedroom clock. I told him I couldn't get a response from her and called 911. It was now 2:55 am. Only three minutes had passed since I woke up! God, it seemed like an eternity! The officer said something into his portable radio and in a few seconds another officer appeared, a female.

The male officer backed out of the bathroom and the female officer went inside. She called out to Betty. "Miss. Miss. Madam." She turned to me and asked, "What's her name?" I told her. She began speaking to her. "Betty, please answer me if you can." She grabbed her radio and said something into it. I couldn't understand what it was. I was standing near the main hall when I heard footsteps. A female EMT was coming down the hall. The female officer got up and moved away from Betty when she arrived. The EMT asked the same questions as the officer and I gave her the same answers.

A dog started barking. Oh hell, it's Bonus, my daughter's dog. I forgot about Melody. Just then she opened the door of her bedroom and asked what was happening and at the same time trying to silence the dog. I told her I had just found her mother on the bathroom floor and called 911.

She looked into the bathroom at her mother lying on the floor. The EMT had taken a bath towel from the shower enclosure to cover her body.

Melody put her arms around me and started asking a lot of questions. What had happened and why hadn't I awakened her? What were the EMT's doing? I answered her as best as I could.

The female EMT pulled out a breathing tube and tried to insert it. At the angle Betty landed it was impossible. She mustered enough strength to roll Betty over on her back. As soon as she did she cursed. I didn't hear her well enough to understand exactly what she said but she quickly followed it up with a call to her partner. She yelled "CODE BLUE! CODE BLUE!" into her radio.

No one has to work in a hospital for two years as I did to know code blue means cardiopulmonary cessation. Melody squeezed me real hard and started to cry and mumble. I held her close. The male officer asked us to move back out of the way and make room. Another EMT appeared with a wooden stretcher. It was comical in a way but he couldn't make the turn at the offset to get the stretcher into the bathroom. He finally figured out how and got the stretcher inside.

The male police officer asked us to come with him so he could get some information. It was a distraction tactic. We went through the entry hall to the kitchen and sat at the breakfast bar. The officer took out a notebook and found an empty page. I gave him my name, my wife's name and my daughter's and our social security numbers, address and phone numbers. This officer was nervous and unsettled. He himself didn't seem to know what to do.

I saw the EMT's carrying Betty out on the stretcher through the kitchen window. The officer we were talking to was becoming more nervous and anxious. The female police officer called out, "Let's go!" The male officer told us to stay home and wait by the phone. Dumbfounded and in total shock, we did as he said.

After they left my mind began to fill with thoughts of death, insurance, inheritance, children, grandchildren, relatives, phone calls, funeral arrangements, travel arrangements, phone number listings, wedding vows, sleeping alone, raising grandchildren alone, being father and mother to three daughters, two son-in-laws, bills, work, savings, bank accounts, lawyers, doctors, police, EMT's, wills, medical records, drivers licenses and credit cards. The list it seemed, endless. Not one thought formed in my mind, or Melody's, to following the ambulance or going to the hospital, an action that should have been instinctive.

It was shortly after 4:00 am when the phone rang. The voice asked, "Mr Campbell?" I said, "Yes?" And the voice continued, "The hospital needs you," I said, "Okay," and the caller hung up. *Isn't that terrific* I thought to myself? *Call and don't give your name.* I relayed the message to Melody in partial disbelief. She stated flatly, "I'm going too!" I wouldn't have debated that comment for anything.

I changed from my sweats into a shirt, jeans and shoes. My mind was still foggy from the events of the last hour. We got in the car, backed out of the driveway into the street and drove to the hospital. I don't remember looking both ways to see if the road was clear. I recall faintly I didn't see any lights coming or going so on instinct I kept moving.

The hospital was only a block from the house. Without thinking I pulled into the handicapped parking spot at the front door. Before I switched off the engine a cognitive thought occurred to me that she would have been taken to the emergency room. I told Melody to stay in the car. I put it in reverse and backed out into the street. I had never been to the emergency room before so I hesitated briefly in looking for the directional sign. I saw it and headed for the access road.

I recall pulling up into another handicap slot and thinking I shouldn't park here. This space is for the handicapped. I wasn't the handicapped individual. A handicapped parking placard was hanging on the rear view mirror. It was issued to Betty following her foot surgery. And besides, at this hour who was going to argue about this car being parked here? Back in California, any member of the family driving for a handicapped person was allowed to use it. In Idaho the handicapped person is the only one allowed to drive and park in handicapped spaces. What the hell I thought, it's her I'm here for - to hell with the law!

We got out of the car and walked up the ramp towards the emergency entrance. I pulled the door open and let my daughter go in first. We went inside and looked around. We didn't see anyone in the waiting room or the hallway. There wasn't a receptionist or a nurse or anyone to talk to. Just then a nurse appeared from an exam room. Melody went to her and explained that her mother had been brought in by ambulance about an hour ago and wanted to know where she was. The nurse, in a deep German accent, told her, "She expired. The body was already cold when it was brought in. I'm sorry."

My daughter turned to me, grabbed me and wept uncontrollably. I too joined in mustering what strength I could to keep from falling down from being weak in the legs. I became stuporous myself. I didn't know whether to cry, yell, or scream. I chose to cry. Mostly I think from the grief my daughter conveyed to me.

We stood in the hallway for a short while exhausting our shock. We moved out of the hall and into the waiting room. The nurse followed after us. We sat down. The nurse stated they didn't know who she was and it was customary for relatives to accompany patients to the hospital at times like this. Melody explained the police officer had told us to stay home and wait by the phone. The nurse commented that was dumb. The hospital would need to notify the next of kin immediately.

We told her we got a phone call from a female voice and came right over. She stated she thought it was an EMT who had called. The nurse told us that the doctor worked on Betty for forty minutes but was unable to revive her. We asked where he was and could we talk to him? She told us he left after he was unable to revive her.

She repeated they didn't know who she was when she was brought in or who to contact. I repeated our story and told her again a woman's voice had called the house and told me the hospital wanted us here. The nurse restated she thought that might have been the paramedics who called but it was still normal for the family to accompany the patient to the hospital. She wasn't understanding our plight.

I explained yet again the police officer told us to stay home until the hospital called which is what we did. She was stuck on normal protocols overlooking our personal condition of shock.

I slowly began to realize I made a major screw up. Damn, I thought latently, yes, I should have come to the hospital when her body was removed from the house and to hell with the officer's comment! Damn! Damn! Damn!

"Where's my mother's body?" Melody asked. We were led to a treatment room. Betty was still lying on the gurney with a sheet pulled over her. I fell apart. The white sheet brought back vivid memories of two stillborn sons in tiny white coffins being lowered into the ground in England.

My knees went weak and I became very unsteady as I gazed upon the form of my wife under the sheet. I reached for and sat down on a nearby rolling stool before my legs let go. I sat beside the gurney, found her right hand, placed mine on it and cried uncontrollably. I was alone.

I sat there holding the now lifeless hand of the best friend I ever had as the tears poured from my eyes. The one person in the whole world who had known more about me and my habits, ideals, abilities and traits than anyone. Before me lay the body of the woman I loved for over 29 years and my best attributes. Her memory was so keen and sharp I needn't remember anything, she, who forgot very little.

Now what was I to do? I couldn't remember. My memory lay cold and blue upon the gurney before me. A colder feeling than that of loneliness or lifelessness; engulfed me. Now I had to fend and do for myself. I didn't know how any more. I had left almost every decision up to Betty to make. Now it was up to me, alone, to make the most crucial of all decisions - a funeral service. Of all the things Betty and I discussed about death and dying, a service was never planned.

My daughter stood by my side crying on my shoulder. Not even her presence could allay my feelings of loneliness. I don't know how long we stayed but exhaustion from crying finally overtook the tears when they finally stopped. There wasn't too much water left.

Betty wasn't wearing the first wedding ring I gave her on her right hand. With the grief of the initial shock being swept away by a flood of tears I asked my daughter to see if her second wedding ring was still on her left hand and if it was, to remove it and give it to me. She walked around the gurney and lifted the sheet. She muttered, "Oh God." as she picked up her mothers hand and removed the gold ring from her finger. It didn't want to come off but she succeeded in removing it.

I asked her what the "Oh God." statement was about.

She replied, "Her hand and fingers are already turning blue."

I felt dumb. But I hadn't noticed. The tears and the subsequent swelling around my eyes had distorted the colors I was seeing. I took the ring from my daughter and placed it in my pocket. I didn't want it on her finger when she was taken to the mortuary.

Mortuary? Funeral Services? Autopsy? I had to collect myself. There were surreal problems to be taken care of right away. Some cognitive realities were beginning to return. At long last I told my daughter it was time to leave. There was nothing further to be done by staying. We had to find the nurses station and find out what arrangements were to be made to take Betty's body to a funeral home.

We went up the hall to the nurse's station at the main entrance. I asked the nurses if the final cause of death had been determined and would an autopsy be in order. We were told the doctor of record hadn't stated the final cause of death. The coroner would make that determination. I was stupefied. In all the incidences I ever encountered with death I had never been in a situation where someone other than a medical doctor declared the final cause of death.

Okay, I thought to myself, *I don't know what the Idaho statues are as it applies to death but I'll play your silly game. So where is the doctor or the coroner for that matter? Someone, anyone, tell me, what was the final cause of death!*

I was also told the need for an autopsy was would be at the discretion of the coroner unless the family had a specific reason for it. My chief concern was the insurance companies rebuking a claim for any insignificant reason they could muster to avoid paying off on the life insurance policies. Besides, I had deep reservations about what the contributing cause might have been since her wishes were to be cremated. Once the body was destroyed by fire there wouldn't be any evidence left, just her written history and the medical reports.

I knew in past years insurance companies would investigate every death before making payments. Investigations could take up to six months or more. In the meantime families had to endure severe financial hardships and extra court costs. I had a faint recollection of a judicial decision some years back wherein the courts decided the insurance companies had 30 days to honor claims. If they suspected foul play they had to go to court to get permission to delay payments. Further, if they wanted to investigate every claim it could not be the basis for withholding payments. If they chose to investigate, it was their right, but not at the expense or grief of the families. At that time insurance companies were investigating deaths by natural causes routinely. The court ruling further determined this was an exorbitant waste of time and effort, which was being passed on to policyholders as overhead and was grossly unnecessary.

The nurse who told us Betty had expired asked if I had a preference for a funeral home where the body could be sent, if not, Summers Funeral Home was next in rotation. I must have given her a queer look askance because she continued to explain there were only two mortuaries in town and if the family had a preference that would have to stand.

I told the nurse I had no preference. Summers would be fine. We made the arrangements for a mortician to claim and store the body until I could regain my sensibilities and make funeral arrangements.

The coroner arrived shortly after I signed the papers releasing her body to the mortuary. We sat in the main hall and discussed my wishes and concerns.

After nearly an hour of discussion I relented on an immediate autopsy. The coroner satisfied himself the final cause of death was cardiac arrest. A history of thrombophlebitis was also present as a possible contributory cause. There was evidence of a pulmonary embolism prior to cardiac arrest.

In summary, Betty did not suffer or know what happened. Clinically death occurred with the same impact as a 30-caliber bullet. She was dead before she hit the floor. She was still 'breathing' when I found her because she landed in a position that did not completely cut off her air supply. When the EMT rolled her over to insert an airway device that movement cut off the airway and cardiac arrest was immediate. She may or may not have had an aneurysm prior to cardiac arrest. Only an autopsy would conclude that. The issue of an autopsy was left open until I had more time to consider our discussion. With nothing further to say or do we went home grief stricken and mentally exhausted.

At home I began to look around and take stock of what to do next. Notification of next of kin was in order. It was now 5:45 am.

I'm not so cruel as to call and wake family and friends at this early hour and on Saturday to boot to tell them Betty died this morning. That would have to wait until a more respectable hour. The next step for us was to go back to the bathroom and see what kind of a mess there was to clean up.

There were some small bloodstains from where her head had been lying. The stains in the carpet would have to be dealt with. I asked my daughter to get some cleaning solutions so the stains wouldn't set. A small amount of blood had seeped through the throw rug and penetrated the wall-to-wall carpet. It was a very small stain.

I began to pick up and collect the debris left by the EMT's, cotton swabs, syringes, sanitary wrappers, breathing tubes, gauze and the like.

I was trembling, weak, confused and disoriented. *Dear God*, I said to myself, *what do I do now?* I felt totally helpless and inadequate, all our discussions about death and dying. Who would be first? What would the survivor do? The estate? The will? The funeral? The funeral. The funeral! Yes, the first to die was to be cremated, then what? Internment? Where? When? The ashes of the first of us to die would be placed in the coffin of the second to die. But where do they go in the meantime? Betty, what did we decide? Did we decide? I couldn't remember! My remembering had died with her. She who remembered everything! I didn't have to remember. What did I have? I had nothing!

Melody returned with some cleaning solutions and rags. I left the stains for her to do while I turned my thoughts and attention to the bedroom.

The bed sheets were still damp. I noticed the trashcan had been moved. When I looked inside I saw some sputum in the bottom. I reasoned that sometime after I had gone to sleep Betty must have thought she was having an attack of indigestion too. In reality she was having the onset of her heart attack. When she got up to go to the bathroom she collapsed. The angle at which she landed precluded her windpipe and air supply from being cut off completely hence the snoring sound I heard when I woke up. By whatever set of circumstances or events she had no chance of surviving, nor did she know what happened or when. That was something to be grateful for.

Melody interrupted my thoughts. "Dad," she said, "the stains won't come out." I sprayed them again and I'm letting the solution set for a while."

"That should be all right." I replied.

"When are we going to start calling the family and our friends?" she asked.

I glanced at the clock. "Not before 7:00 am. I need to find all the phone numbers. Boot-up the computer please. I'll have to run a phone number listing from the data base."

"Are you all right Dad?"

"No, I'm not. I can't remember what to do next. Nothing. My mind is blank." My frustrations were renewed.

"Let's go get the phone numbers and figure out who is calling whom," she suggested.

"Yes," I agreed, "it will take a little while to sort that out." I need some time to clear my mind. I'm not hitting on all cylinders at the moment."

We went up the hallway, towards the recreation room as we called it. I needed a list of family and friends to contact. All the names and phone numbers were in the computer's database. This was going to be rough, real rough.

Melody booted the computer and I tried to focus on how to run the program and initiate a phone number listing. After several fumbling attempts we finally succeeded in extracting all the names and phone numbers from the file. I decided I would call the family members and let my daughter call our friends. In that way we could trade phone calls and recover from our announcements. It would be more merciful to us this way.

I started down the list giving the names of friends to Melody and reserving my other daughters Tammy and Wendy, my mother and my sisters for myself. The worst problem I faced was telling my older daughters, the parents of two newborn grandchildren; their mother died this morning, Wendy's, a scant 8 days after her baby was born. God give me strength, I don't want to make these phone calls.

I explained to Melody, "We'll wait until 7:00 am local time for the recipients. I don't want to wake anyone from a sound slumber on a Saturday morning with such bad news too early. Waiting any longer would be too difficult for us. It's 7:00 am back east now but I don't have any phone numbers for that side of her family. The closest group is in Denver and I only have one number to call. It will have to do. I can't hold myself together long enough to talk to all of them. I'll call Arlene first and let her pass on the news to the rest of the family there."

To my daughter's dismay I did wait until dawn before calling. I couldn't share her concept of calling immediately. I was not of the opinion anyone should be awakened from a sound nights sleep to receive such bad news on a Saturday. Morning would come soon enough and we had lost enough sleep for everyone.

An hour of eternity passed before 7:00 am. Reluctantly and with a great deal of anxiety, I reached for the phone to make the first call. I began trembling again. Damn push button phones! The buttons won't stay still. The phone on the other end rang twice and a female voice answered, "Hello?" I heard a female voice say.

"Hello Arlene, this is Gene in Idaho. I'm sorry to call so early but I have some bad news. Betty died this morning." At that statement I lost control of my emotions. The remaining words I thought about using stuck in my throat, choking me and I began to cry uncontrollably.

Arlene's voice on the other end stammered, "Oh Gene, I'm so sorry. I don't know what to say." She waited patiently for me to regain my composure then asked, "Can you tell me what happened? How did it happen?" I told her briefly of the events of the last three hours and we concluded our conversation with an understanding she would notify the family members in the Denver area. They would contact me later as to their individual and collective plans.

This call was typical of how most of the announcements to each and every friend were made. The calls to my two daughters living out of state were, by far, the most painful. When I called Wendy, Chris answered the phone. He was notably curious why I should call so early on a Saturday morning. When I told him Betty died this morning he assumed I was talking about my adoptive mother. My daughter on the other hand knew differently and her screaming in the background confirmed it.

When I called Tammy she answered the phone. I asked her where Brian was. She told me he was already at work. I asked her to ask him to call me-it was urgent. (I couldn't bring myself to tell her of her mother's death while she was home alone). Brian called back from home a little later. I told him the sad news he relayed the announcement to Tammy and the screaming in the background began again.

The memories of the calls I made to my daughters out of state still haunt my days and nights. Their screams in my mind are as vivid today as they were on that fateful morning.

I told and retold the story of the events of this night far into the morning. Everyone who was told asked the same questions. We told them all the same or similar stories. After the 20th time I think I began to muddle some of the details. By noon I was mentally exhausted.

I was asked by several of our friends if I needed something, a sedative, to get sleep with. I declined their offers. "No," I commented, "I'd go to sleep, start dreaming about this morning and have no way to wake myself from reliving the horrors of this night. I'd sooner learn to live with it. I must live with it."

Betty died early on a Saturday morning. Notification of next of kin was easy enough, notifying a few select friends was also easy enough. However, notifying my immediate supervisor and co-workers proved a more difficult task. Most would be impossible to locate over the weekend. That meant waiting until Monday morning. Not much time to tell them about the funeral arrangements for a Tuesday or a Wednesday, let alone the death of my wife. As events unfolded I wasn't able to locate or notify my co-worker's of Betty's death until Monday morning.

On Saturday afternoon a family acquaintance arrived and assumed the duties of travel coordinator. I allowed our friend to make the travel arrangements for my daughters and their families living out of state. I gave her my credit card and my blessings. In Betty's words, "She done good."

On Sunday morning a friend of the family stopped by to see what we were doing. "Nothing," I said, "until the family arrives, then all hell will resume with hugging, crying and pain." She inquired about us having breakfast. I declined. Food for the body wasn't high on my list. I had no appetite anyway. But she would hear none of it. The body needed nourishment to sustain itself and to give the mind sustenance also. She took us out to a church breakfast. Her suggestion was blessed and proved necessary. Sitting around the house waiting wasn't good for us, a stable meal for the first time in 24 hours was needed and the exposure to other people was essential.

Tammy and Wendy and their families arrived on Sunday, one in the late morning, the other in the evening.

Teri, a real close friend of Betty also arrived on Sunday in the afternoon. The two of them were so close she refused to believe Betty had died. It took Melody and I three calls to convince her Betty's death on Saturday morning was true. Upon her arrival she summed up their friendship as, "First we moved from behind each other to different streets, then to different towns, then to different states and now she's gone forever."

I wasn't so sure the physical distance was the most important observation. "To my way of thinking," I said to her, "Betty is now in a place to watch over all of us at once without regard to physical being."

* * *

Our funeral arrangements were complicated by the time and day of Betty's death, the need to inform out of state friends and family for a gathering, a funeral service to be taken care of and all of them returned to their own lives. (I learned later death paid many visits to town that day and the next two. A total of eleven people died between midnight Friday and noon Monday. Both mortuaries were real busy.)

On Monday morning Teri and I went out for breakfast. She felt it was necessary for me to get away from everything and everybody for a couple of hours. It was a correct thing to do. Sitting idly by and waiting for something, anything to happen is bad mental health. Our conversation centered on funeral arrangements. What had I done so far? Where is the funeral? Have the cards been ordered? Her list went on.

I hadn't done anything. To begin with, I reminded Teri she had died very early Saturday morning. With both husband and daughter being in shock, a next of kin notification list to be handled, a family gathering to be arranged and friends to be notified, there wasn't time left on Saturday to plan any sort of funeral services. The day ended and the funeral directors went home.

The mortuary office was closed Sunday. Death may not take a holiday, but mortuary officers do need a day off. So here we were on Monday morning, a body in the mortuary and no plans for services. Woe was me!

Our first order of business was to find suitable clothes for the services. Next was an appointment with the mortician to have a date and time set for the services, after that the memorial cards had to be selected and printed, then prepare for the service itself, ask a priest or chaplain to conduct a service and notification of the service arrangements to my employer, my family and our friends. From these decisions my family and her could make return travel plans.

We finished breakfast and left the restaurant for home. Melody helped me with the clothing selection. We decided on everyday wear type clothing. Nothing fancy. She was to be cremated so there was no reason for finery clothing to be used. With her clothes in my hands, Melody and our friend Teri, we left for the mortuary.

We turned over the clothing to the mortician who handed them to an aide and gave instructions to prepare for a family viewing at 1:00 pm.

I began looking through the card selections, first selecting a suitable announcement card, then a memorial card and lastly some suitable saying or poem indicative of our life together or her life in particular for the announcement card.

Both Melody and Teri assisted me with the final service arrangements. I made a few select decisions about cards and front covers then Teri took over when I encountered a poem in the memories catalogue relating to "friends" and I lost all my composure. The poem read:

MISS ME - BUT LET ME GO

When I come to the end of the road
    and the sun has set for me
I want no rites in gloom filled room
    Why cry to a soul set free?

Miss Me a Little - But Not Too Long
    And not with your head bowed low
Remember the love that we once shared
    Miss Me - But let Me Go.

For this is a journey that we all must take
    And each must go alone
It's all a part of the Master's plan
    A step on the road to home.

When you are lonely and sick of heart
    Go to the friends we know
And bury your sorrows in doing good deeds
    Miss Me - But let Me Go.

* * *

Monday evening Chaplain Thompson stopped by for a second visit and to offer his services as the presiding chaplain of Betty's memorial again. I had declined his offer on the first visit because I couldn't handle all the problems and decisions being thrust upon me initially. Neither Betty nor I were devotedly Christian people, certainly not the every Sunday worshippers and I felt a Christian service might be out of order. With my mind now relieved of much of its burden after a family bereavement session at the mortuary earlier this afternoon I consented to his proposal. There was merit as well as friendship coupled to his offer which was worthy of his presiding over the service. Both he and Betty were good friends and when Betty was elected chaplain of the chapter's veteran service organization he presented her with a chaplain's cross that she wore to the monthly meetings. It was a source of pride and comradeship between them. Betty would certainly approve. It made sense in more ways than the two reasons expressed here. In Betty's words "He done good."

    The funeral itself was held on Tuesday to avoid further complicating matters for return travel arrangements by Teri. She would leave the morning after the funeral. Her departure would be a heart wrenching experience for me.

Seeing her again after three years and at the parting of her closest friend redoubled the grief I endured. For all the special talks the two of them had together it seemed Teri's only contribution other than troubles was to oversee her best friend's funeral and services. It seemed to me a short fall of their friendship. I hoped Teri would be able let Betty go - as the poem in the memorial had read. They were closer than sisters.

The services were kept simple. They had to be, not a great deal of planning went into it. I'd heard of prearranged funerals before and had never paid much attention to them. Given my miserable experience I wish I had been less of a skeptic as a young man. When the chips came down the burden was too great for me to hold up to. Immediately following Betty's funeral I planned my own services and filed the instructions with my new will. My daughters know where the instructions are located. Better for me, better for them.

Friends Depart

I was asked about a reception following the funeral. For myself I declined. I wanted the funeral to end the grieving and the suffering. But as my head cleared it became apparent the reception was more for the friends of the family than the family itself. Friends needed a respite from the shock and the service. They were touched by death whereas the family was embraced by it. The reception would make their pain and offering easier.

It was held in our home and attended by 125-150 friends of the family. Our two grandchildren made the reception more pleasant, each was passed around, held and cuddled, by everyone who could get an arm around him or her. They were the only bright light in the day.

Most of the friends of the family were local residents. When they left that afternoon to carry on with their lives I turned my attention to family matters at hand. I was still feeling aloof, partially on air, as if I had not yet got my feet back on the ground again.

In four short days 150 volunteers waited on my family and me hand and foot. The time had arrived for me to begin taking stock of my situation and begin taking care of my family and myself. One immediate chore loomed before us. Where to store all the food left over from the wake? There was certainly enough for a family of eight (my children and grandchildren) for a month if they were all staying that long. The clean up committee told me they would return in three hours. However, it wasn't really necessary.
I/We needed something to do - idle hands and that sort of thing. Our minds also needed a rest from the impact of grieving. Thank goodness I had two large freezers. We packed

and wrapped and stored everything perishable. It was a good undertaking. It was beneficial too.

My First Psychic Vision

The morning following Betty's funeral a strange event happened. I was awakened by what I felt was a kiss on my forehead. I opened my eyes and looked around to see who it might be. To my surprise I saw Betty standing beside the bed. She was clad in the clothes I had her dressed in for the funeral. The sight of her presence muted me. Before I could utter a word she said two things to me, "You done good," and "You'll be all right." Then she vanished.

Whether what I saw was real or in my minds eye I'm unsure. I recall distinctly what I saw and what I heard. It was real to me. Whatever opinion others might have is strictly that, their opinion. Psychologists and psychiatrists will long deliberate the significance of this event and to that they are entitled, however, I am not concerned with their opinions.

The expression "You done good." was a standard phrase Betty used frequently. Admittedly, I had doubts about the funeral arrangements we had made and I felt this statement was targeted at it.

The expression, "You'll be all right." was another standard phrase Betty also used frequently. It may also have been deductive reasoning forced out of my subconscious mind or foreknowledge by her apparition I would in fact be okay. I was in need of both statements.

Whether either statement or the event itself was real or imaginary who is to say? My mind and body and soul received comfort from the event be it real or imaginary. If it gives peace of mind and peace of body to the human experience, why analyze it?

* * *

In the few remaining days before my older daughters left to return to their homes we all went to an attorney and reinitiated my/our wills. I did so as a precaution against the possibility I might decide to remarry. "That which was created from our marriage is the inheritance of my children and must provide for them," was my mother's philosophy. I took it to heart and to an attorney.

I queried the probate process for Idaho with him. Since the wills were reciprocal probate was not absolutely necessary. I decided to deal with the court later in a few more months, after a thorough, clear-headed examination, of what life in solitude would offer. To me, there was no immediate hurry for this task.

My Family Departs

Tammy and Wendy and their families left on Friday. Both departures were gut-wrenching experiences. If not for Melody and my adoptive mother living with me I'd still be at the airport window crying for them not to go.

After they left the three of us went to dinner to discuss the events still pending and living arrangements.

Melody felt the responsibility for "raising Dad" fell upon her shoulders. I assured her it did not. Her mother had left me quickly and too soon, but getting on with living, even alone was a fact of life I would have to deal with. I asked my adoptive mother Betty to remain with us for another week and when she was assured we would be all right to carry on with her own life. She agreed.

The following Friday my daughter and I were left alone to get on with our lives. Betty's parting was another torment to me. I was becoming accustomed to having her around, but she was correct, she had to get back to her family and friends and we had to get on with our lives.

Ashes to Ashes

On the first Monday following the funeral the mortuary called to tell me Betty's ashes were back from the crematorium. Melody and I went to claim the urn and its contents. I felt somewhat apprehensive at the prospect of claiming and taking the urn. To my surprise I was completely calm and relaxed at claiming her remains. I was at peace with myself - literally. I also reexamined my feelings at cremation for myself or being interned in a coffin in the ground with Betty's urn at my side. I decided for myself then and there cremation would be better for me.

The urn itself is beautiful, made of solid oak and laser carved with a country scene of a lonesome oak tree beside a pond of still water and with a flight of ducks passing a rising moon. It is the sort of view Betty had great joy experiencing in real life.

When my adoptive mother Betty saw the urn she asked if I had bought one for myself so ours would be matching. (We had discussed cremation for me as an option after picking up Betty's urn.) I had thought about the prospect of matching urns but not to the **fac**t this particular urn may not be available when my time came. I decided to purchase another one exactly like it while they were still available.

I called the funeral parlor and explained my desires. The director made arrangements for another urn to be ordered and for me to pick it up. When the urn was delivered I went immediately to get it. I was tingling with anxiety. How do I hold and look at my final resting place and not feel nervous? Again - to my surprise, I felt a great inner peace within myself sitting in the lobby of the mortuary holding the urn that would one day contain my ashes.

Another man, sitting in the lobby opposite me, asked me about it. Specifically, "Who is the urn for?"

I replied, "It's mine," and I said it with all the calmness of a man at peace with himself and his world.

"It certainly is a beautiful urn," the gentleman replied back.

"Yes it is," I whispered in serene voice.

Chapter 6

The First Few Months After

"Where we once walked together, I now walk alone."

Sleep Deprivation and Living Alone

Sleep deprivation soon convinced me I couldn't sleep alone for the rest of my days. I blame the doctor who long ago suggested I could wake up one day sleeping next to a corpse. My subconscious habit of reaching out, searching for a still-warm body during sleep time had subjected me to this horror in ways neither he nor I could have conceived so long ago.

My capability to adjust to living alone would be possible, I thought to myself, although highly undesirable. I'd resolved to myself I could live the rest of my life alone if I had to, I knew I didn't want to and therein lay the difference.

* * *

I slept very little from the weekend Betty died and into the next twelve months. The most sleep I could obtain was 2 hours a night for the first two months. (My friends and family told me later I awoke crying in the wee small hours of each morning for the first week following Betty's death and the funeral.) I might retire by 1-2 am and be wide-awake and in tears by 4 AM. I would stay in bed until 7:00 am or 8:00 am and contemplate longer on all those thoughts and tasks I had only flashes of in my mind on that fateful morning.

Sleep deprivation consumed my existence for six months after Betty's death. Even after such an apparently long length of time I could barely manage 3-4 hours each night. By the end of the first twelve months I was still only able to get 4-5 hours of true sleep each night. I would spend the remainder of eight hours, lying, simply resting my body. My mind would still be going full tilt at my memories, my problems, my depression and dealing with being alone.

Initially it was filled with thoughts about death, police, EMT's, doctors, wills, life insurance, probate court, inheritance, children, grandchildren, relatives, funeral arrangements, travel arrangements and later wedding vows, our marriage pact, sleeping alone, raising grandchildren alone, being father and mother to three daughters, two son-in-laws, debts, work, savings, bank accounts, lawyers, medical records, memories, love and anger.

My mind would ricochet from one topic to another and back again and then start with a new one without solving the present problem. My ability to concentrate on one problem at a time was useless. My mind ran the gamut of my problems every morning. I was looking for answers but my mind chose to supply them at a time of day easiest for it without regard to my physical need for rest and relaxation. Minds work that way.

* * *

While all these thoughts still occupied my mind the concept of maintaining a journal (a recommendation of the presiding chaplain at Betty's funeral) was added. "The journal," he said, "will provide a written record of these events and when read by your descendants will make you a real person in their minds, more than a picture on the wall or a faded memory. It will also assist you in your grieving and provide an outlet for your innermost thoughts and decisions." I gave in to his recommendation and I'm glad I did. A year after Betty's death I took those thoughts on paper down from the closet shelf to read them. I was both amazed and perplexed by all the issues that permeated my mind during those infinite moments.

* * *

My most perplexing problems after the first four weeks was whatever shall I do now? Betty was gone and I was left to carry on. Whatever should I do? My conclusion was to do as we both had planned. I had a vested interest in the decisions we made while she was alive. Her passing didn't end my desires. They weren't made strictly with Betty's desires in mind. So I chose to pursue them. A major problem for me to deal with was our marriage pact.

Our Marriage Pact

The first two weeks following Betty's death my mind dwelled mostly on our marital life together. I recalled our wedding vows taken so long ago. I reviewed every word in my minds eye and our discussions involving those vows after she developed the blood clots. While we were young and foolish the world offered no task we could not accomplish. We considered ourselves as immortals. As time passed and our health conditions worsened our visions of immortality faded.

We came to realize after the formation of her blood clots and with death's hand forever around the doorknob, a life of raising children if we had any and alone, would not be practical.

My job in the Air Force carried an undue amount of risk itself. Working on missiles was not a glory job. In those days it was quite deadly. The specter of death and disability loomed like a ghost over every event. The propellants and oxidizers used to fuel those "birds" was a deadly combination, inside or outside the missile itself. With sudden death or permanent disability a grave possibility we made a pact of sorts, the survivor should remarry or at the very least not spend the rest of his/her life alone or in solitude. We felt and concluded, the wedding vows died with the death of either partner. There was no moral sin in seeking another life with another man or woman.

I went over that particular pact a lot in the days and nights that followed her passing. The pact that we made from the outset of the revelation her medical problem could take her first. We had agreed, regardless of who died first, the survivor should remarry.

I was also influenced by other comments that added support to our pact.

I had survived the missile field and its dangers for the most part. I didn't get away Scot free, alive, but not totally in the prime of health. Betty survived her childbearing years. Our daughters were full-grown and all graduated high school. One went on to advanced education. Added to these circumstances was the number of comments and observations made by several friends that I was still a young man, 50 at the time and could still meet another woman to share in life's adventures, 50 years old and still a young man, another dichotomy or a mind-bending issue? Was the need to remarry really necessary? I wasn't sure, but I felt like I wanted to be. An associate at work cemented the idea for me.

My colleague had commented, "If you want to get married again it must mean your first marriage was a good one." That particular statement stuck to me with the veracity of super glue. No matter what I thought or did I couldn't shake it.

With this observation and this comment coupled to our wedding pact about remarriage, I felt justified in at least looking. I could always change my mind and give in to staying single. I allowed myself to go looking.

★ ★ ★

My quest, if I could call it that, began a short five weeks after the funeral, from the end of the path of life Betty and I had taken. She had picked her friends pretty well, so I contemplated looking through them first for someone more akin to my feelings, understanding, experience and education.

I started with a cursory look at which of Betty's friends were radiant with her and widowed and still single. There was one woman, Mamie; I thought might be a good companion for me if she was still available, I didn't know. I would have to make a point to see her and talk to her. The last time I saw her she was still single. She was an attractive woman for her age and not strictly in the physical sense. I had an appointment to see my doctor for my quarterly exam the month after Betty died. When it was over I decided to drop by and see her. See how things were going. Since she hadn't attended the funeral, it would be another pretext to call on her, sort of visit and see what surfaces.

Driving the interstate towards my exam my mind was filled with thoughts of both women. Betty and Mamie, one deceased and the other alive. During the trip Olivia Newton-John sang "I Honestly Love You" on the radio and my mind filled with the intertwining thoughts of both women. I began to cry at 65 MPH.

Who was I crying for? Both I believe. My best friend had left me. Perhaps a new best friend was before me? I pondered if I should inquire directly about her marital status and her presupposed interest in me at the beginning of our meeting or allow the conversation to develop naturally? I decided to let it develop naturally.

In the very beginning of our visit she told me she had met and married a man recently. It was a lengthy and funny tale. (She's a chatty person.) At the conclusion of her story she inquired of me where Betty was? I told her Betty had died a month ago and the news silenced her. It became evident to me she hadn't been told. I went over the details of Betty's passing with her. I left a very sad Mamie standing at the banister in front of her office. I walked away slowly feeling dejected and sad. Deep in my heart I wished she would come after me, tell me her marriage story was a dumb joke. But she didn't. By the time I reached my car I felt my best opportunity for a new best friend had slipped by me.

A Second Psychic Reflection

A few weeks after the funeral, I developed enough cognitive ability to concentrate more fully on the events of the previous month. I gave particular thought to why I had been awakened so suddenly on the morning Betty died. The conclusion I arrived at may be unsettling to a lot of people, but in light of events I cannot draw any other conclusion.

I had been asleep for perhaps two hours or more (Sleep studies show this is the deepest part of human sleep. Thereafter, sleep becomes less intense until the waking moment). It was somewhere in this transition I believe Betty herself, by some unknown force or ability, forced me to wake up. I remember waking with the suddenness of an electric shock. Over the span of our 29 years of marriage and more recently at the reaccomplishment of our wills after moving to Idaho, Betty had remarked at the signing of our living wills she wanted this will very much. It was her greatest fear to be mentally trapped in an incapacitated body while it was kept alive by artificial means.

Betty was an educated and intellectual woman. She could not, nor did she intend, to be kept alive in a vegetative state. With those collective discussions instilled in my mind, I believe she somehow knew waking me was an all-important event.

I had found her on the bathroom floor making snoring sounds and nonresponsive. How long had she been there? It was totally unknown to me. She may have laid there for two hours or more. I literally slept through whatever happened to her and when.

I further believe if it had been possible for the EMT's to resuscitate her, she would have been a vegetable. It is by these circumstances I have come to believe she somehow woke me to assure her ultimate death and in doing so accepted her physical life on earth was ended.

* * *

Another perplexing and troubling nonevent arose which disturbs me even today and as I noted in my journals. When I made up a collage of pictures to hang on the wall below Betty's only formal setting at age seventeen, I came to realize two very important pictures were never taken, a photo of Betty, Richard and I together shortly after he was born, one to compliment the grandmother, granddaughter and grandfather photo of Betty, Heather and I and - most importantly - no family photograph of Betty, myself and our three daughters together.

I had a recent high school reunion photograph of the two of us together and snapshots of the three girls together, but none of us - together - as a family. There was but one photo of Betty with our three daughters, provided as a birthday gift before we departed Lompoc. A dichotomy of sorts, when I stop to recall the countless number of photos taken with the father missing in commercials I had seen over the years.

With this void planted firmly in my mind I took yet another look and self-examination of our nonrecorded life together. We were married in a federal court building without any regalia. Betty's mother and the judge's secretary witnessed the ceremony. No photos, no friends, no family gathering, no invitations and no reception - nothing usually associated with making memories. That itself left me with a greater emptiness than being widowed. I had my memories and little else recorded to show my own grandchildren in their older, more mature years of our early life together. I wanted nothing of pomp and ceremony at our wedding when we were married, but now, looking back in hindsight, I regretted not having something of a more formal occasion on record. I had given up a future of faded memories for the present. I assured myself if the eventful occasion of another marriage was to present itself at some future date I would be less inclined to "elope" again.

Returning to Work

I spent the first three weeks after the funeral at home alone - thinking - and perhaps too much, following Betty's death. My friends were back at home and work. My two oldest daughters and their families were back at home and work. My youngest daughter was back in school. My adoptive mother was back in her world and I was home alone in mine. Not a good situation I felt. I decided it would be best for me to return to work and soon.

I went to visit my supervisor. He offered me another week of leave but I declined. Sitting home alone for another week wouldn't do me any good. Going back to work, being around people and getting my mind and body back into some creative purpose was, I felt, better for me. He may have been correct in offering me additional time for grieving but I was already emotionally drained by the events of the last three weeks and wanted to push the pains aside for a renewed purpose in living again. I needed people to talk to, not four walls. I needed work in my hands, not memorabilia.

Associates who had not seen me since the funeral and were concerned for my health and mental well-being again slowed the process of resuming work. I worked very little because I was constantly getting caught up in many one on one conversations day in and day out about the causes of Betty's death. Most of these talks were healthy; a few were not. Those unhealthy talks being the conversations with people with comparable illness'es and paranoia's of their own.

The Throes of Being Alone!

Of all the items I initially thought about in those fleeting moments after discovering Betty lying on the bathroom floor I had sorted out or taken care of the most immediate events first. Making the out of state phone calls to notify our children, relatives and friends; Letting local friends make the travel arrangements for my daughters living out of state. Contacting the insurance companies; Making the funeral arrangements; Putting Betty to rest, Seeing a lawyer to settle the estate; Reinitiated my will; Paid the outstanding bills, medical and mortician; Changed the names and beneficiaries on the savings accounts, bank accounts and credit cards; Obtained copies of her medical records and returned to work. Those tasks took a month to accomplish.

Next I had to resolve the lesser material problems and issues of being widowed. That being disposal of her clothes, sorting through her jewelry and personal keepsakes and deciding whether or not to keep or sell the house and furniture and automobiles. She had also had left behind voluminous amounts of unfinished hobby crafts, hand made rugs, quilts, crocheted items and books.

I felt at odds with myself, unsure of what to do. What to keep, what to sell, what to dispose of and what to throw away. Some of Betty's personal items seemed to be a betrayal to get rid of.

With all these earthly items before me, and the last image of Betty on the morning after the funeral in my mind, and her statement 'I'll be okay,' I still felt hollow. Perhaps she was right, but to my way of thinking, I must be the only person who didn't realize it.

I decided to wait a couple of months for my grieving to subside more, to do more research and a lot more thinking over what final courses of action I should take with her earthly and personal items.

* * *

With the immediate problems taken care of I turned my attention to one last bittersweet task. Christmas was approaching.

Normally this meant Betty writing 25 or so letters and mailing out 75-100 Christmas cards. This year the task fell into my hands. I wasn't too sure what to do until I got a timely family newsletter from a distant friend of the family. I decided to reciprocate with a newsletter of my own.

This is an excerpt of what I eventually wrote and mailed out with those Christmas cards.

Campbell Family Idaho Newsletter Circa 1992

Greetings to family and friends everywhere,
Newsletters like this seem to have caught on as a popular way of sending out Christmas cheer and synopsizing the past years events without getting into an extended letter writing session. I thought this year I would join the parade.

This year has been a roller coaster ride for my family and me. As you may have surmised by now I am writing this year and not Betty. For those of you whom I was not able to contact I must tell you Betty died Oct 17 this year of cardiac arrest. She was 45 years old. We were married for 29 years and had just celebrated our anniversary Oct 4th. Her passing was very unexpected and quick. She did not suffer nor did she ever know what happened. Betty was cremated and her ashes are resting above the fireplace in our home. Our daughters Tammy, Wendy and Melody and I are grateful for the telephone calls, sympathy cards and visits from our family and friends whom I was able to contact. I have enclosed a remembrance card to those who could not attend or I was unable to contact. Betty left behind her husband, 3 daughters and 2 grandchildren, both born this year, Heather was born 21 Jun and Richard was born 9 Oct. Betty and I went to see both grandchildren the day after they were born. The family is comforted and I thank God she at least saw and held them both before she died.

Melody graduated from High School this year and started vocational education. She is studying Administrative Accounting and will graduate Sep 3, 1993. She was recognized this year in the United States Achievement Academy, a National honor roll. She plans to remain at home with me through 1993 and then move out to independency sometime in 1994.

Wendy and Chris live in Novato, California near San Francisco. He is in the US Navy assigned to the Aircraft Carrier USS Abraham Lincoln. They plan to retire to Mountain Home when his career is done.

Tammy and Brian live in Victorville, California. He works as a security guard and moonlights in retail sales whenever he can. They plan to move to Mountain Home sometime in 1993.

As for me I plan to go ahead with the plans Betty and I made while she was alive. I will retire from Federal Service in 1997 at the ripe old age of 55. When you hit the speed (age) limit you ease off the accelerator but keep on going. Thereafter, I plan to become fully involved in grand fatherhood. I have my own workshop behind my home and will devote most of my time to woodworking, emphasizing grandchildren projects, home repair, remodeling and furniture making. In my spare time I enjoy attending auctions and work as a volunteer with the local veteran organizations. I will also continue to bowl as long as my health permits.

Betty and I planned a Tour de California for the Christmas holidays. I will still make the trip starting Dec 20 however Melody will accompany me and the trip will be shortened to allow her to return in time to resume classes Jan 4th.

Afterwards Melody and I will settle down to an established routine of our own and we will all begin a new year with a new accord.

Happy Holidays from the Campbell Family

Discussing the Emotional and Physical Demands of Death With Friends From Out of State

Two months after Betty died I did take the loop trip to California with Melody. The plans were made and I felt there was no real reason to cancel it.

This would be the first Christmas without her. It would prove to be a very emotional time and trip.

I had altered my leave plans from work so Melody could accompany me. It was no time to be alone, at home or away. It was my decision to make the trip, see the family and friends who had not been able to come to the funeral and explain face to face, in person, what had happened to their satisfaction and to enjoy a Christmas holiday with friends and family as much as possible.

My daughter's help with the driving gave me time to read, grieve and meditate. While she drove I read a book about being a widow. In the book I could feel the widow's pain and relate to her misery. We, the author and I, shared a level of understanding. I was upset when I got to the end of the book and read the epilogue. The author had died five years before. Another teardrop fell. I was unhappy again. I was so touched by her person I had wanted to write to her personally.

Christmas vacation 1992 was a bittersweet experience but it did prove to be very beneficial. A lot of goodbyes were uttered, to the places Betty and I went to together more than the people we knew. I had included a few personal niches in the tour where we spent some quality time together. I grieved and cried a lot at those places. For the family and friends who could not attend the funeral I had the opportunity to see them, to share their thoughts and allow them to express their feelings of Betty's passing and explain in person my future plans.

My daughter and I celebrated Christmas six times in less than two weeks in 1992. I am now a firm believer Christmas is a one-day a year event and is best celebrated that way - like birthdays. I'm not sure I could tolerate twelve days of Christmas every year. The experience was interesting and enjoyable but I found it to be mentally taxing. The trip itself was pleasant and exciting but we were both physically and emotionally drained by the time we came back home.

I spent the first winter of my discontent touring California, seeing and talking to friends and family members on my side of our marriage. The need for it was undeniable.

Betty's side of the family in Colorado however also had a need, a need for me to visit, to talk and maintain contact.

It would take over a year but I would finally set aside my day to day concerns and leave for Colorado in May 1994 to see Betty's side of the family and to visit and answer any unresolved questions. There would be few questions left.

The long delay in going to Denver after Betty's death would turn the occasion into a social visit more than a grieving one. My time however would be well spent.

Discussing the Emotional and Physical Demands of Death with Clergy and Friends Locally

My time spent with clergy discussing my loss and bereavement was two and short. The chaplain who presided over Betty's funeral service gave me sound advice on maintaining a journal, which I did. At another time, I met with another chaplain as part of my work duties shortly after Betty's passing. We discussed estate planning and surviving spouse problems at length.

I wish I had taped that conversation (it lasted 2 1/2 hours) and had it for reference, but minds don't work well when dealing with death. Neither did I make notes. If I had had the journal idea planted in my mind before speaking with another chaplain I surely would have made some good notes. Part of the reason I believe my mind fails me in recalling our lengthy conversation was because I had already taken or planned to take every possible action and step timely and correctly in dealing with the loss of my wife according to him. I won't rehash previous subjects here and now and the rest are explained in detail in the remaining chapters, but I became assured that not all bereavement conversations lead to becoming a reborn or renewed Christian in a solitary life-after-death existence. The chaplain did provide me with solace without the "salvation" talks many widows and widowers shy away from. I did come to understand an estate planning discussion with an ordained priest, chaplain, reverend or other clergyman during bereavement had been necessary. My mind needed peace and salvation from every source.

* * *

In the four months after Betty's death I discussed at length, the concerns of several well-intentioned friends and family, locally and on the road tour. Some of their concerns and questions bordered on paranoia from my perspective, beginning with, "Was Betty's cholesterol high?" among many others. From these conversations she'd died of heart disease, smoking, cholesterol, too much red meat, heredity, family tradition and blood clots. I observed the cause for an individual's concern was usually derived from their personal worries about their own illnesses and phobias than her actual cause of death.

She died as a result of cardiac arrest. As to what actually preceded it, we'd never know because I did decide against an autopsy. It wouldn't have served any useful purpose except to possibly provide a basis for insurance companies not to pay off, a long legal battle which would only serve the interests of the legal profession and cast doubt over the medical profession. And where would I be then? Bent, broke and frustrated. She died of cardiac arrest. Case closed. The immediate family knew of the probable leading and contributory causes. No one else had a right to know more than that. I soon edited my story with friends and co-workers to a condensed version.

Prologue 2

Betty's passing left me with many paths to follow, so many in fact I compared them to the "All roads lead to Rome" saying but in reverse. I felt as the hub of an aged wagon wheel, all paths extending outward 360 degrees from center. I was dizzy at the problems presented at my feet. Unlike shoes, few spokes led to a specific solution. Those that did were dealt with immediately. Others, more complex, became extended in their being. My search for answers was comparable to a man sinking in Mississippi Mud - hoping for a passerby with a rope to remove him from the quagmire.

I spent the first four months of my widowhood resolving my problems as quickly as I knew how. I had much to learn and little time to dwell on the learning curve. The problem counts manifested themselves much as germs multiply - geometrically. I became impatient, with my surroundings and myself.

The funeral was dealt with systematically, it had the greatest importance and time was not a luxury. With the aid of many friends Betty was laid to rest. The survivor issues were mine and mine alone to deal with. I had no learning to guide me. Experience would be my only teacher. Councilors I had plenty, good and bad, the topic and person dictated the adequacy of their advice and my willingness to accept it.

My continuing narrative will not dwell on standard protocols, those dealing with the acts of life and death, much of which has been written about exclusively by female writers and were encapsulated for me in Chapter 6. Part III focuses on the emotional turmoil I encountered in the first months after the funeral. I was thrust into several complex circumstances in those four months. All of which were blended as they occurred. For simplification I have chosen to deal with each problem individually by separate chapters. To intertwine them as they developed and over various periods of time until each was resolved, would overwhelm and confuse the reader. They certainly did me.

Chapter 7

Reaching Out Against the Loneliness

"For death to have any significance grieving must be experienced.
Suppressing grief will only make it last longer."

The Pendulum Swings

Unbeknownst to me joining the support group would cause me to suppress my personal bereavement for a year. Instead of completing the grieving process alone and living through the torment it brings I would reach out against the loneliness for a soft shoulder - and not one to cry on.

The Support Group

A week after I returned to work the news of a new, single again, support group starting came across my desk. By this time I felt I was pretty well over Betty's death but perhaps, just perhaps, there was still something I was missing from the grieving process. I wasn't an active churchgoer. I didn't drink either so that wasn't an option. (Being single tends to drive people towards one or the other especially at times involving death and divorce.) I'd talked and listened to family and friends at length. Now I felt would be a good time to listen to others who had walked this mile and learn first person about all the aspects of being alone again in a couple world and from strangers who had experienced these feelings too. A support group seemed the best compromise. Not too left, not too right.

Before attending the first session of the new group I made a vow to myself, if I was the only male there for the support group I wasn't staying.

To my complete and utter surprise there was only one female present. Three men and one woman attended the first session. What a comforting start! Our introductions were kept simple. The councilor informed the attendees this was a support group, not a dating service. She imposed one rule - "What you do here, what you say here, stays here." The rule was simple and straight forward enough.

The group grew to five men and four women in four weeks. The meetings were short and to the point. Open and interactive conversation was permitted. If you chose to say nothing and just listen that was fine too. No one pressed anyone into speaking.

We were informed of other support groups outside of ours. Most involved lengthy travel and were highly structured. One in particular caught my attention. I read over their pamphlet that was brought to our meeting. I had already experienced the first nine of their twelve topics, those being the customs and traditions associated with laws, business and bereavement. I was interested only in the last three; dating, fidelity and the matrimonial condition - to remain single or remarry. I felt I had the rest under control. Their last three sessions however wouldn't take place for another two months. What good would they do me then? I wanted those answers now, not in two months! I decided against joining the other groups. The three remaining topics of interest to me I could bring up in this group. Among them would be personal ads.

I sort of lead the group discussion into personal ads the next week. I had seen and read some of the ads in the newspapers. I had reservations about trying something that far removed from my cultured upbringing. There was however some interesting prospects. Some women were homebodies who are what I felt I needed and someone more akin to my desires and feelings. The topic having been presented for discussion I sat back and listened to the younger, more experienced, attendees. When the session ended I went back to work to ponder the days discussion. Later that night, in the comfort of my home and in privacy, I reread the page containing the personal ads in the newspapers then outlined a personal ad of my own. I highlighted the positive and negative points I had to offer. It looked a little this.

> Who wants an old fart of 50 who doesn't smoke, doesn't drink, doesn't want any more children, nor pets, lives a sedate lifestyle, attends auctions at every given opportunity, enjoys music, movies, television, is an inactive exerciser, has emphysema, hypertension, muscle spasms, gout, costochondrasitis, hernia, hemorrhoids, halitosis and bad dentition; is kind, gentle and considerate; woodworker, model builder, painter, reader, writer, bowls and fishes once every 29 years.

Betty would say yes, another woman, perhaps. In looking over the ad I figured I didn't have much to offer to another woman through advertising. I set the ad aside while contemplating other "meeting" alternatives.

I developed the trait of sitting and listening and observing the active members of the support group banter topics around the table, played the devil's advocate with them then and myself later. Participation wasn't my strong point. My main objective in attending the sessions was to broaden my own knowledge through other people's experiences and to compare their problems and solutions with my own. I observed I made most of the right decisions for the right reasons and a lot sooner than other widows or widowers in the same position. Still, there were bridges I had yet to cross. The overpowering question became; could I live with another woman, be it as a friend, a significant other or a wife? Could I find another female companion?

Examining the Facets of New Potential Relationships

In my "just looking" phase of seeking out another woman to be a companion for me I examined my prospects. From where would I start? The beginning of the end, an old flame, a childhood sweetheart, do I seek out a woman totally opposite from me again? Or do I require she have more in common with me a second time around?

Strange as it seems these points of interest were the topics of discussion at the next support group meeting I attended.

I wasn't spouse hunting at this meeting but I took the opportunity to examine more closely the issues I would not normally think about. (You can't sit or stay home and wait for an available or eligible female to knock on the door. You must go forth and meet them where they are.) From within this small circle of diverse women I could evaluate some pretty out of the ordinary situations. Could a future relationship be with another civilian or a military woman, officer or enlisted, older or younger, attractive or plain, physically fit or ill, emotionally stable or angry or even bitter, with or without children, fertile or sterile or change of life, religious or nonreligious, out of love or loneliness, admiration or sympathy, widow or divorcee? It was a small circle but dynamic. Real questions. Real problems. Real life.

The group discussion on companion hunting gave me a lot to think about and a lot more to ponder. My mind however still dwelled on our marriage pact, the comment of my acquaintance at work and with passive thoughts about my age.

And beyond this group of women, another, a personal column, the supermarket, a shopping mall, a diner, a recreational place, a social event, a chance meeting? Will God help?

Will God help? The question reminded me of a punch line in a joke I had heard long ago about a couple in a boat who were caught up in the eye of a storm. They had been spotted in their duress by a hurricane hunter aircraft. A radio call for help was sent out. A seaplane arrived first to rescue them. They declined to leave with the pilot saying, "God will help us." The plane left without them. Next, a submarine arrived with the same offer of rescue. The captain was told, "God will help us." The sub left without them. Soon the couple was overtaken by the storm and drowned. At the pearly gates Saint Peter asked them what they were doing there? The couple relayed their tale of despair to Saint Peter. He responded by telling them God knew they were in trouble and provided a plane and a submarine to save them, what else did they expect? I resigned myself to try to recognize help in any form, not just a preconceived form.

The Types of Women I Chanced to Meet Over the Next 12 Months

Between January and December 1993 I met several different women and dated a few of them, some of them were support group women, a cautious experience at best.

My dating skills were a good 30 years old. The group discussions on current accepted methods of meeting single people in this, my early stages of single again life were helpful, coupled with previous group discussions about examining new potential relationships I ran the gamut of my queries. Slowly and surely I discounted particular women for particular reasons.

The prospect of a military wife, officer or enlisted, was disconcerting. I had packed my bags and family steadily for 20 years in my own military career. I had been to 11 states and 2 foreign countries. I was burned out with travel and had a greater need to take root someplace.

The few older women I met all seemed to have adult children still at home.

The younger women I met were too young, a decade or more, with their biological clocks ticking way too loudly. The prospect of starting a second family lacked appeal.

Physical stature played a small part in my determinations.

Could I take care of a sickly woman? That was hardly likely considering my own state of health. It depended on the nature and stage of her illness. What I needed was a woman who could take care of herself and could take care of me. That was a more important issue.

Mental health and personal attitude played a significant part in my decisions. Most of the women I met and dated were emotional wrecks. Between death and divorce that's not unrealistic. But how they dealt with those emotions was reason for concern. Few of them retained a positive outlook on life.

Religious outlooks could mean trouble for me. I'm not a profoundly religious person but some latitude must be given. I shared my religious philosophies with some women and for the most part found the differences to be a barrier. My own family consisted of Nazarene, Presbyterian, Catholic, Church of England and as yet to be determined. We lived happily together so long as no one confronted another member of the family taking a position their religious preference was the right one.

Love or loneliness, it was difficult to differentiate one from the other. Two lonely hearts seeking companionship don't see the difference. Love is blind can then take on more than the one, traditionally accepted, meaning. Time and dating would determine which would be a motivating factor for being with another woman. These same facets held true for admiration and sympathy.

The singular difference between a widow and a divorcee was permanence. In death the separation is a done deal. In divorce the other mate is still available. S/he can reappear at any time if they are so inclined. As to the never married before woman, unlikely, I met only one and from my perspective there was a personality problem.

The Influential Women I Met and Their Major Attractions

The women I met and dated in the support group were Dora, Maria and Angela.

Dora was the first woman I met following the death of my wife. She was a welcome influence in my life while I sorted out the depressions of being widowed. Dora was a happy go lucky woman despite the fact she was trailing Elizabeth Taylor and Zsa Zsa Gabor for the most marriages. Through all the rough and tumble events of her broken marriages she still retained a sense of humor. (I personally felt she was searching too hard for a companion.) I saw through her the prospects of getting married again and pondered a younger second wife and for a time, even to her.

The traditional barriers that existed in the support group meetings did not arise during our dates. We spent a few evenings together tracing family ancestries then we would go to a diner for coffee and desert and mellower conversations. There we discussed more openly our deeper feelings and desires for a companionship but never with each other. The subject ran submerged like a submarine and didn't surface. The lady I spent those evenings with was rewarding and pleasant. They made her attractive. To my chagrin though she possessed a shortcoming as a potential partner. She had never had children and her biological clock was still ticking. In my advanced years I couldn't commit myself to rearing another family.

Maria was a widow who had been home bound for years and going to school since her husband's death. He had died a few years back after an extended illness. She was still carrying the headstone of death around her neck when we met. She attended only two of the same sessions as me in the early months. She never said much in them so it was hard to access her problems. I only knew she was a widow and attending school. In a later, summer session, she would finally let out her feelings and the tears that flowed would have powered Boise for a day. (It was from that session I came to understand her grief never started, let alone could it end.)

She was a good conversationalist and a delight to be with. We talked nearly exclusively about living alone, dead spouses and learning to date again. On our second of two dates I discovered she was really dating me to inquire about a widowed friend of mine whom she was also seeing. I told her what I thought I could reveal about him and not lose a good friend. I admired her and felt I was missing out on an excellent relationship for myself; however, happiness is its own reward. They became happy together so I kept my feelings for her from her.

Angela was a physical compromise between Dora and Maria. A tall, medium built woman in stature and body, an English redhead with pale blue eyes and an accent that could crack ice. She was about to become legally separated when we met. Between her stature, personality and at home lifestyle I felt totally at ease in her presence. I also felt an ancestral closeness with her. She was a pedigreed Englishwoman, I, one-quarter Englishman. One of my overseas tours in the military was spent in England and as I learned, in close proximity to her childhood homestead. I wasn't sure, but I also felt I had met her once before, at Vandenberg AFB in California.

I observed Angela to be a very angry woman. And with good reason, at least from the points of view she brought into the group meetings. Her husband was to her reasoning an infidel. Her son was a teenage terror. I knew she was hurting a great deal. I became aware through our private discussions she had had problems with drinking previously. In my adoration I tried to help her with it, little realizing, I would further cultivate the trait to drink.

I purposely avoided calling or asking for dates after meeting her because of the mental anguish she imposed on my mind from our weekly meetings through the support group. I perceived her to be a warm, gentle, loving person with some rather distant concepts about families. We began dating nearly exclusively after she moved from her house to an apartment and before her legal separation. I helped her to move, which later proved to me, to have been a major error on my part.

The women I met outside the support group were Ellie, Rosie and Mamie.

Ellie I met via the church route. She came to visit once a month and to check on my grieving processes. She was a young and very pretty woman with a lot to offer but our differences in religious beliefs was a barrier. Those visits convinced me a relationship with a woman of her deep-seated devotion, at any age, would not work. Her closeness to God, young as she was, was too profound. I summarily dismissed the idea of settling down with any woman of her religious depth as not possible. There was nothing personal in my reasoning; I just couldn't bring myself any closer to her than as a member of the church.

She stopped by for a last visit before going to Canada. I held her hand while thanking her and wishing her well, perhaps a lot longer than was necessary but then her hand was warm and the feeling of a young woman's touch was welcome. I had hoped I had convinced her that her presence and her words were welcome but I had already believed, lived and experienced them. While her concepts of God and family and mine were similar, hers were based in regimented religious beliefs and mine were less focused and more personal concepts. I assured her I would be fine in the future. I didn't use labels but the meaning was the same. I wanted to hug her but it would have been improper. I was sure she wanted to hug me also but I had reservations of what her motives might be. Still in all, I was filled with a certain peace, not of the mind or the spirit but of the body at our parting.

Rosie was a widowed woman of advanced years. One of those petite, never run out of energy types even toddlers couldn't catch. I had difficulty keeping up with her. She was a handsome woman, very alert and very intelligent. Her husband had passed away some years previous. She also had a forty-something child still living at home with her. We saw each other at least once every three months, sometimes more often. We enjoyed each other's company and on rare occasion dated and dined together. I felt (we never discussed) she was chasing me a little. She was a grand woman, however, she was 20 years my senior and the prospect of interring another woman to eternity in a decade or less caused me to shy away from her. (She was not the only widow I knew living in this arrangement but it did make me stop and think about the prospect of a much older woman and a middle aged child still living at home.) I concluded both were undesirable.

Mamie was another widow I knew for a long time and was closer to my own age. Her husband had passed away some years previous also. On my trips to Boise I would stop by and visit her from time to time throughout my widowhood. We would meet and dine and talk together, a sort of one on one support group therapy. She could talk about death and divorce and loneliness with equal fortitude. (Our relationship became an intermittent event throughout my widowhood.)

The inevitable comparisons between these women drove me nuts!

School Girl Sweethearts and Flickering Flames

While dating all these local women I reflected upon childhood sweethearts and flickering flames from my past. A few stood out above the rest, girls and women. Each one possessed their distinctive physical attributes and personalities. I recalled who they were and why I was attracted to then. The problems to be surmounted were, where are they now? Were they available?

* * *

From my childhood years, school years and military career, I thought about the teenage girls and women and the twenty something set of my generation whom I had met and came to adore.

The first girl to leave a mark on my mind was Bonnie. She belonged on a pedestal in my eyes. And well she should have, for it was from a distance I admired and adored her. We were the same age, we attended the same schools and classes since kindergarten and I watched her grow up and develop into womanhood. She grew to medium height, had brown hair, brown eyes and an hourglass figure. Physically, by the age of 18 she grew into the epitome of what I felt would be the ideal anatomy in a mate for life. Alas, I could never bring myself to talk to her. I was dumb struck in her presence so I hardly got to know her personally.

The second girl to arouse my feelings and interest was Joanie. Physically she was a more full figured girl with blonde hair and blue eyes. I saw her in a bowling alley one day when I was walking home. The distinction we both had something in common, bowling, added to our dates and meetings. She attended another school in another town so dating and courting her meant more of a challenge. I did my best. We dated on occasion and she even went to my prom with me. Our relationship ended when her father's company moved them to another state.

The third girl to make an impact on my life was Ruby. If Aphrodite had descended from the heavens, this must have been the form she took upon earth. She was beautifully proportioned in height and weight, with auburn reddish brown hair and the softest brown eyes this side of velvet. I had the good fortune to date her but once. But in that date she burned a hole in my heart forever. Beauty aside, we developed a rapport on an intellectual and conversational level. She set a new standard for the girls and women after her to follow. Unfortunately, her parents couldn't abide me.

The fourth girl to influence my life was Ruthie, another full figured girl with brown hair and blue eyes. She was much smarter than me which I felt was a positive thing. I realized at an early age education and intellect got more people ahead in life than hard, physical work, which was as much as I was good at. It would take smarts as well as labor to make a relationship work. Alas, my interest in her was in vain, I discovered she was betrothed to another young man and reluctantly stayed away.

The fifth girl to have any meaning to me was Linda. She was a reversal of what I had physically admired in the female form. A slender young girl with black hair and black eyes, she took on the dark side of a relationship. I had several dates with her but when it became apparent she wanted to rule the roost and the rooster I flew the coop. Sharing was what I had in mind in a relationship, not slavery.

The sixth girl I met was a composite of the previous five. Her name was Betty. A well figured young girl of the sweet sixteen tempo. She had blonde hair (until I turned it gray) and Sinatra blue eyes. We courted and dated more intently than I had in any of my previous relationships. Our initial meeting was influential of our future life together. I happened to ask her for directions one day when I was lost and she never missed an opportunity to give me directions again or for the next 29 years. Yes, I married her. Yes, I robbed the cradle. Yes, I raised her to suit myself. When she died I lost the best friend I had.

Flickering Flames During Our Marriage Also Surfaced

The first twenty something woman in my life was Carmelia. I met her while married to Betty. A woman of fantastic beauty, charm and intellect, I almost wished I had met her before Betty. She had a slender build, almost petite, long black hair and green eyes. My off chance meetings with her resulted in jealousy by her husband and Betty. As much as her person entranced me I told her I would not leave my wife for her. Later, she was divorced by her husband after being sterilized, the result of a tumor. If I had believed for one moment, happiness of a higher plane could exist by being with her I might have left my wife and family for her. Reality bites however and she wasn't worth the cost. I remained married to Betty and very happily too. The "affair" brought us closer together.

The second twenty something woman in my life was Judy. I met her at a convention. She was a married woman also. I felt and believed, her marriage was one of convenience, little if any romantic substance was involved. She was petite in height, weight and stature. We met on a philosophical level during a convention. We became fast friends. I was very impressed by her philosophies and her positions in her approach to her work. When I contemplated all my facts and fantasies in another possible wife she scored perfectly. As with Carmelia, reality bites, maybe in another lifetime.

Where were they now? Unknown. None of the high school sweethearts I had attractions for attended our high school reunions. My last contact with any them was at graduation. Were they available? Unlikely. Tracing family history is difficult in itself; old sweethearts from a high school would be more difficult. As for the flickering flames it would be better to let them die out.

My obvious conclusions to looking for school day's sweethearts and flickering flames - they wouldn't have worked as marital partners then - they wouldn't work now.

* * *

My trip through memory lane brought an interesting observation to my mind. I'd met and known several girls and women in my life. But what made them so distinct in my mind were the phonetic sounds and the spellings of their individual names and the impact each of those names had in my life. In my postpartum depression of being widowed I continued my self-examination of this observation.

Call it petty or coincidence but the girls and women who had or were having the most impact in my life had names ending in "a" or "ie" or "y". Those that ended in "a" had caused me trouble and grief despite my adoration for them. Those whose names ended with the phonetic "ie" sound were good for me but not completely. Those whose names ended in the letter "y" have had the most profound and positive effect on my life and me. I would have married any of them under the right circumstances. I did marry one, Betty.

I noted in my sauntering desires and relationships with Linda, Dora, Maria and Carmelia they were not completely forthright in their feelings. Linda hid her feelings behind a seemingly sharing nature while really looking for control. Dora said she wanted a family and towards the end of our dating implied it wasn't necessary. Maria was looking over my shoulder at a taller, more suitable suitor. Carmelia lived in the illusion I would divorce my wife and family just to be with her. These became my negative flings. Angela seemed to break the general observation of women with negative effects for names ending in "a," at least on the surface.

My relationships with the other girls and women I'd known were for the most part favorable. Bonnie, Joanie, Ruthie, Ellie, Rosie and Mamie. Each separately became the models of desirability I would seek in a lifetime partnership. Bonnie provided the initial concept of the physical qualities I would later seek in a wife. Joanie showed me how common likes and dislikes are necessary for day-to-day living. Ruthie possessed an intellectual attribute. Ellie was simply too young. Rosie was too energetic and not living alone. Mamie was a good friend who maintained the memory of her deceased husband too intently.

    My more intense and satisfying relationships were with Ruby, Betty and Judy. I have loved and do love each of these women dearly and each for different reasons. Ruby was the first and infinite love of my life. We acquired more affection for one another in one weekend than most married couples do in a lifetime. By the time I met Betty I was resigned to the fact that a great physical adoration would not survive the bonds of matrimony. Friendship must prevail as the first prerequisite for a marriage to last. To marry primarily for the physical satisfaction meant when it ended, the marriage would end too. Betty and I started as friends; later we became lovers. The outlook I developed was when the physical love diminishes; the friendship would still be there. The philosophy worked quite well. 29 years later our children were the only kids in school with both natural parents still married to each other and still living together. Judy was a platonic, fleeting love of mine. If not for both of us already being married, we could have made excellent partners.

Chapter 8

Embracing Another Woman in My Life

*"It's taken a while, but I can laugh again.
The pain is still there but-it's not dominate any longer."*

Seeking New Companionship

Loneliness soon developed into solitude for me. After many sleepless nights and daydreaming days I had resolved fairly well I should try to engage in a relationship with another woman whose own interests were more like my own. Over time the other women I saw and dated during the first year of being widowed had been discounted for various and sundry reasons. A few months of loneliness and learning how to court again helped me to make a selection. It was me and my desires or the lack of them that steered me in Angela's direction. I found in her presence I could laugh again, with her and more importantly, at myself. The laughter removed the domination of the pain I was experiencing. I certainly needed this form of relief from my grieving. Following my self-examination of the other women within the support group and a few encounters outside the support group I had narrowed my beginning choice down to her.

Deciding Upon a New Love in My Life

I was happy in her company or around her person. She became attractive in my setting. Within the spectrum of guidelines I set for myself, I felt the better facets for another companion in my life existed in her. She was a civilian, near Betty's age, attractive, midway between fit and ill, given to fits of temper, no children living at home, no prospects of having more and nonreligious. Love or loneliness and admiration or sympathy would be resolved by dating. I became apprehensive in time with this decision but I felt strongly both for and against a continuing relationship with her. Whatever I felt was wrong was subliminal and evaded my attention and my reasoning.

What were the main attractions? To me, her mannerisms, personality, accent, manner of dressing and stature. She had an ethnic background similar to my own and from what I observed so far we had a good deal of personal history in common. I didn't doubt there would be as yet unknown differences, but only time and being in each other's company would bring them out.

We had more in common than my other female contacts but how much more was there to learn?

Our relationship had began too soon, developed too fast and took me a few weeks to slow it down, but I managed. I knew were both hurting a great deal, her from her estranged husband and me from the loss of my wife. Our new relationship should be slower in developing so neither of us would feel we were rebounding.

But was *I* on the rebound? Was this woman to be my next true love? Angela seemed to be a sincere and devoted woman. Her conversation and body language dictated as much. So what effect did this woman have on me? In retrospect, I lost a night's sleep the first night after I met her. I didn't see her again for another week and slept better. I assumed I would not see her again. The thoughts I had about her passed from my mind as a dream. But another week later I saw her again and I lost two nights sleep. Our third meeting cost me three nights sleep and a lot more mental anguish. Our fourth meeting resulted in a week of anguish and confusion for me. I had certainly lost enough sleep over thinking about her (as much as I had with Betty). And I lost even more sleep with each new encounter. She seemed to be giving me old, familiar desirability signals. Did I really love her or was that yet to come? Did she really love me? These were the questions I kept asking myself and no answers came forth. I was caught in the vortex of my emotions.

I'd lost what little ability I had regained to concentrate since our introduction. Her being preoccupied my mind. I'd go to sleep thinking about her…dream about her all night…and I'd wake up in the morning from dreaming and resume thinking. She'd gotten pretty deeply into my mind. My stomach hurt the rest of the day following a meeting alone with her or in the company of others. My feelings she needed a kind, gentle person in her life labored on my person. I felt I was that person.

I shared my dilemma with my adopted widowed mother in those early months following Betty's death. I explained to her how I met Angela. I couldn't put my finger on it but I believed it was reciprocal. And I thought Betty would approve. They were both alike in many respects. There was no physical resemblance between them but otherwise they were very similar. Her husband had asked her for a divorce before we met. She had agreed. I knew the situation was crazy but I couldn't shake the feelings I had for her or her situation.

I told my adoptive mother Betty how certain scenes in the movies we had seen together and parts of those stories sounded like parts of our lives; how bits and pieces of each of those movies made for slices of life as it pertained to our lives. Namely, a widower eventually meets and marries a divorcee.

I asked her other nonrelated questions such as; How much did Betty know when she told me I'd be all right before vanishing altogether the morning after the funeral? Did she come back just to kiss me good-bye or to reassure me of my future? Would she be happy for me? Was I imagining more to this than really existed?

My adoptive mother couldn't answer most of my questions. She did warn me however this affair was coming too soon after the death of my wife and I should take more time to finish grieving, if not for the whole traditionally accepted, full year. I personally felt I had completed grieving. The balance of the full year concept seemed a waste of time and energy. I was personally convinced this lady was good for me. I made a silent decision then and there to ask Angela to my home for some light entertainment on Saturday.

The invitation was for an evening of dinner, television and conversation. She arrived early and I had to let her sit alone briefly in the living room while I finished some chores and food preparations.

    Angela had not been to my home before or attended one of my popular nickel tours. During the tour of my home I made a Freudian slip by commenting, "How would you like to have to clean this house?" She replied she could do it. (Later, I was to find out through one of my daughter's this statement can be taken by some women as a proposal leading to marriage. It depends on the woman and her upbringing.) I showed her around the house pointing out the woodworking projects I had accomplished. She had noticed a wooden box on a bookcase shelf while waiting for me, commented how pretty it was and asked had I made it also. (She thought it was a jewelry box and in a funny location.) I told her it was the urn that held Betty's ashes. It had been her wish and our agreement, to be cremated and when my time came we would share the new upper mantle over the fireplace of this house. The concept gave our daughters comfort.

    Angela left shortly after the tour. She passed on the dinner, TV and conversation that I had planned for the evening. I dined alone, in front of an opaque TV screen and talked to myself about what I might have said or done wrong. (She would tell me later the sight of the urn disturbed her. She felt funny being in the presence of a deceased woman's remains.)

* * *

My interpersonal relationship with Angela began shortly afterwards, much too soon for my friends and family's way of thinking. Not too soon I felt for me. We enjoyed each other's company and reveled in the similarities of our joint ancestries. We found happiness and comfort in each other's presence. Should that have been so wrong? Time would prove how wrong the relationship was for both of us.

A statement made in the support group by one of the women as told to her by her grandmother was - "One man for four seasons. If it doesn't work after that it never will." The expression "Waiting a year" losses flavor when set beside the four seasons concept. This saying solved two problems for me. I would use this piece of advice to my own purpose. Namely, I would date Angela nearly exclusively for at least one year. In that time I would get to know her better. We would see each other frequently and at the end of that time if our relationship didn't work we would end our arrangement. If our relationship did work I would take it a step further, an engagement and/or living together.

Love is blind it is written. A person cannot understand that expression without the experience. We enjoyed love as we saw it. It was passive and congenial. It would not however become the great once in a lifetime love we thought it should be.

I helped her move into an apartment prior to her divorce, an errant maneuver on my part. It was a quaint little one-bedroom house. It seemed misplaced in the suburbs of town. The architecture was more conducive to a cabin in the mountains. It was very comfortable for a single person or a couple.

I saw her two to three times a week pending their divorce. It was a dumb thing to do. And, of all the sordid stories of men and women whom I'd read and heard about all my life committing this same sin, I discovered the act of seeing an estranged, about to be divorced woman, the easiest thing I would ever do.

I berated myself at length about the dangers, the consequences and the moral implications. For all my self-examinations and arguments, I couldn't find the answer to stopping myself.

I made no assumptions as to the sin I was making. I felt no remorse at the deed. I had an uneasy feeling in the pit of my stomach but nothing there prevented me from continuing to see her.

Our dating together was simple. Most dates were spent in the privacy and comfort of her apartment. We dined in quiet unhurried pleasure. We talked idyllically of companionship, places and family. After dinner she would clean up as I sat contentedly in the living area reading or watching television. Then we would cuddle closely together on the sofa, resume our conversations from dinner and listen to romantic music on the radio before retiring for the evening or I would have to leave. We made for a happy contented couple according to our friends and the associates we met. People we met in public assumed we were married, the judgment being made by our rapport with each other. It was a splendid arrangement with a dark secret.

I observed but failed to relate that Angela would accompany me to special events and social occasions only once. Thereafter, I would have to go alone. I was left dejected and confused by this mannerism. Direct questioning provided no answer. She would say, "No," and that would be final.

Our frequent talks about the immediacy of her divorce drove me crazy. Early in our dating and several times during, I had to talk her out of going to her attorney to get an immediate divorce so we could date openly. I declined her that choice at every opportunity.

What we had was good and beneficial at our beginning, but nothing in our relationship through our early dating I felt, was reason for her to undertake such an irrational act. We had not made a permanent commitment to each other. Should our relationship fail for any reason she would be left out in the cold without me and without her husband's support. I threatened to leave also if she didn't abide in self-preservation. Waiting until the divorce was final was the safest and sanest thing to do. I didn't tell her bluntly, but from our repeated conversations on this topic, I sensed there was something drastically wrong. Not knowing what it was, I resigned not to commit myself to a lifelong relationship until I did. Soon I began to ask more questions of myself than I could muster answers to about us as a potential couple.

* * *

I made arrangements to go to the family history center one night before going to Angela's. When I got home from work I set about assembling my briefcase for the errand. En route I planned to stop by the bowling alley and post the weekly standing sheets. I had dinner at home before leaving and as an act of courtesy called Angela to tell her where I was going and how long I might be. She asked me to come right over - almost demanded (She wouldn't state her reasons for her urgency). I promised I would be over soon but I had errands to run first. She said that would be fine, in anger and she would be waiting. She sounded distressed.

As a precaution I packed an overnight bag just in case it turned into another late night emotional siege. She was given to fits of temper I learned. I felt apprehensive. I was becoming aware our particular arrangement was getting to be a foregone conclusion and she was developing exacting expectations of behavior on my part.

At the family history center all my genealogy leads about her family were empty. Frustrated by 8:00 pm I quit my research and went to her place.

When I arrived at her house she was agitated and drunk and on the edge of paranoia. She calmed down shortly after I arrived. I gave her a stern and loving talking to about drinking. I assured her if she couldn't take care of herself then she couldn't take care of me. She said she didn't realize it worked that way. Even though her mind was groggy with wine what I said made sense. She made a choice to quit drinking that night and it was the right one from my position. We finally poured the bottle and her last glass down the drain. Thereafter we sat and listened to music until nearly 11:00 pm.

I thought from this moment I had convinced her drinking would not be a satisfactory condition in our relationship and made it clear I would be looking for weakness. If her drinking resumed we were finished. She told me she accepted my statements and my conditions about drinking. I made a conscious decision that night our continuing relationship was to develop even more purposely than I previously conceived.

As to her genealogy research I tried, she explained she had given me the married names of women in her family not the maiden names. We sorted those out and I resolved myself to investigate them later without her knowledge.

Later we retired. Sex was brought up. I however could not bring myself to make love to a drunken woman. Just as fighting and making up would not result in sex, neither would drinking lead to sex. That night I began imposing those conditions. I said "No," and made it stick. Reality had to set in sometime.

* * *

After six months of dating I began to assess my relationship with Angela on a family level. She had had difficulty raising her son. Could she handle three stepdaughters? She had induced doubts.

I sat with her son while Angela made a trip to the grocery store one night during the legal separation period. His parents being divorced troubled the young man. I myself being a child of divorced parents listened to his concerns and then related my own tale from my own perspective.

My parents divorced before I was two years old. Over the intervening years to manhood all I heard about the divorce was my mother's point of view. I made no judgment from her statements. I didn't meet my father until I was 20 years old. Then I heard his point of view of the divorce. Again, I made no judgment from his statements. I did however conclude both were right and both were wrong. The bottom line was they couldn't learn to live under the same roof together. At the time of the divorce I was too young to understand any of it. After meeting my father and listening to him, I understood children aren't equipped to judge their parents.

Many years ago, before I met Betty, I picked up a napkin from a bar table and read the sayings on it. Those words written stick with me even today. "Lovers make children." "Children make parents." "If you don't like the way your parents turned out you should have raised them better." Parents do the best they can with what they have in education, experience and love. These sayings I relayed to him.

I admitted to him I didn't know how dumb parents were until I became one. It's an awesome responsibility to create a child and then raise it. They are created through a physical act of loving and raised in an emotional environment. Through it all the parent places a great deal of trust in a child to grow up, become a responsible adult and perhaps, a parent in their own right. As one child of divorce to another I advised him to not judge his parents, "We, (the children) are not equipped for it."

He confided he had resolved his differences with his mother in the last few weeks, "Go and do the same with your father," I advised, "I know what your father did and I understand why. He fell victim to the same feelings of inadequacy I did after my wife was sterilized. I overcame it, he didn't. Now he's paying a price for his error. It's his error not yours (the child's). The torch has fallen," I continued, "don't bend over and pick it up for him. Don't blame him. He must live within his own prison, for as long as it takes him to overcome his pain. Just as a parent cannot live a child's life for them neither should a child live a parent's life for them either."

He asked if I had fallen in love with his mother. "No," I said, "at least not yet." He asked me to explain further and I told him, "She has many of the attributes of my late wife. Physically they are not alike. Their basic similarities are their principles and values. Both women were/are pedigrees, both are of the Old English ancestry and I hold an admiration for the English people. She also upholds many of my own values. I enjoy her person. I think about her a lot. I even dream about her. But I won't allow myself to love her until I'm satisfied I'm not rebounding and the attraction between us is sincere and singular."

Perhaps my statement to him about falling in love sounded ridiculous and I should expand a little. Betty and I were the best of friends who became lovers and in time, and later learned how much in love we had become. Does it still sound contrary? If you marry for physical reasons and that fades away you don't have a basis for continuing the relationship. Divorce is inevitable. But, by marrying a friend the relationship can't fade away. Friendships are enduring. When the sex is gone the friendship still remains. Friends communicate; lovers fornicate, which has more stamina?

I concluded our conversation by assuring him nothing I presently had would ever be his mother's and nothing she presently had would I accept from her. If we were to live together, or even marry, our estates would be kept separate.

My Trip to Silver City

Midway through my dating and near the anniversary of Betty's passing I decided to fulfill my plans to go to the mountains. I spent what would have been our 30th Anniversary in Silver City, Idaho, an old mining town west of Mountain Home in solitude, walking through pioneer cemeteries reading epitaphs, rereading a book on widowhood, reminiscing my past and generally expending any and all traces of remaining grief. Aside from the Christmas trip and the support group it would rate a solid third place as a good decision I made over the previous 12 months.

It was a slow and tedious drive up the mountains to the small mining town of Silver City nestled between the ranges.

It took a mere 30 minutes to tour the town, all seven of the open buildings. There wasn't that much to see or do. Then again, my reason for going was to conclude the last planned event in my late marriage and to sweat out any residual grief that might still be present. I toured the local cemetery. People had been interred there for nearly 150 years. Some of the epitaphs were very moving. Two of them I could connect with in my own life, the passing of a wife and the loss of a child.

I took a book along with me, *Being a Widow*, by Lynn Caine. The book was written by a woman, for women and dealt primarily with the effects of death to women, a gender specific story that had some high points not related to gender. I reread some selected chapters in the book again, there in the mountains, those dealing specifically with death and grieving and when the tears stopped I rested. In between those chapters I ate and contemplated my life as it had been and how it should continue.

I gave thanks for what I had albeit briefly to my way of thinking. The scorecard for October read, 31 positive events and one negative event. I was married in October, celebrated 29 anniversaries, had a grandchild and lost a wife. Not bad when you look at it in that perspective. No reason to allow a single solitary event like death to ruin an otherwise perfectly good month of the year.

I left the town and the mountains early in the afternoon. It was no use staying too long and having to come back down that connect-the-dot road in the dark. I made it back home before sunset in the valley. At the junction to State Route 78 my radio reception returned. A male voice was singing, "Walk On." I felt assured I could. The Ivory pure portion, 99.44% of my grieving was out of me. The .56% that was left would always be there and I could live with that. I was alone and resigned to it. Death would not become such a terrible event as to ruin or rule the rest of my life.

As events later unfolded the idea and the trip was the best idea I had in the 12 months since Betty died. Later that evening I also reread my journal of the events from October 1992 - September 1993. It was amazing what thoughts passed through my mind that fateful day and for a year after and how much I had forgotten.

The revelations of my trip to the mountains were this: The empty nest syndrome goes beyond the absence of children.

It also encompasses widowhood. If you live your life for another person, whether they are a child or spouse or parent and when that person departs your life to live on their own or dies, then your life ceases to have meaning. The moral of my observations: Live your life WITH another person - not FOR another person. The pain of loneliness and grieving are easier to experience. Do not enshrine a deceased person. To do so detracts from your own well-being. Memories are good and sufficient.

My trip to Silver City also decided for me it was time to undertake the construction of a new upper section to the mantle of the fireplace - specifically as a final resting place for Betty's ashes and mine.

I built it with help from my son-in-law Brian. The mantle underwent several design changes but when completed solved my problems. The plywood panels were replaced with mirrors to give a reflective look of the masted ships I placed in front of them. They also took on the imagery of being windows during the holidays when the ship's were removed for Christmas decorating. Galley rails separated the urns from the remaining artifacts placed on the shelving. By its size and weight it took four men to lift it into position and to secure it against the wall above the existing fireplace mantle. It was installed on Christmas Eve.

Chapter 9

Courting Again

"The more we grew together, the more we grew apart."

Self Realization of a Wrongful Affair

My attraction for Angela began in blissful blindness. We were drawn together in great haste much as two magnets are attracted to one another. It's a dichotomy of sorts but the more we came together, the further we grew apart. The attraction began out of loneliness and then in love but really had its basis in sympathy and admiration. For me, dating should have solved the reasons for my attractions but did not. Dating did more to mire my vision than open it.

Still, I decided to propose and to allow a year of living together to resolve the questions I still had.

The Decision to Propose

I spent a full year dating and courting Angela before making a conscious decision to propose. I did it on Valentines Day. I still felt something was wrong but a year of dating had not revealed the answers I sought. My mind was drifting off into fantasyland as to what it might be. My next proposal was to live under the same roof together and thereby establish once and for all exactly what the mystery was and what my uncertainty was about. My premonition it was serious plagued me terribly. The four seasons concept didn't function well during our dating. I felt a courtship might prove more useful.

I was further troubled by the idea if Angela didn't work out what would I do then? Resume dating? Search the personal columns? Go to public places? Attend social functions? Take any reasonable offer that comes along? Or seek solitude? I had developed a deep comfort in being half of a couple again.

Three months after our engagement started my daughter Melody left home. I admit there was some stress and strain building between her and this new woman in my life. It took some time but it became apparent to me that gaining another female influence in my life may have had some detrimental effects on my own family. I felt an ominous power struggle developing. Through the foray she moved out seeking independence. A mite reluctantly I might add and perhaps too soon emotionally.

The departure of my youngest daughter from the family homestead wasn't the only departure in the affair. My eldest daughter and her family also had some bruised feelings. I found out a week after an event there was one sensational personality clash between all of them that brought out an opposing view of the empty nest syndrome by Angela.

Her philosophical point of view about why children should have an impact or influence in our lives kept coming up between us. Angela didn't want her son but I wanted my daughters.

After some clear-headed thought I decided my family to be more important and of more value to me than the haunted desires and philosophies of a newer love affair. I had in an odd sort of way created a love triangle of another sort, this one didn't involve two women and a man. This particular triangle centered on a man, a woman and families of creation.

I set the record straight by telling Angela pointedly she could "divorce" herself from her son at the age of maturity if she was inclined, I, on the other hand, preferred the close and personal bond of my daughters, son in laws and grandchildren. This became a barrier between us. This philosophical point of view was not the problem that plagued me, however, but it was a branch from the real thing.

My Trip to Denver

Three months into our engagement I made the trip back east to visit with Betty's family and friends. It was preplanned and should conclude the grieving process for them and for me in the same perspective as the Tour de California for my family. It would give me an opportunity to see the memorable old places of our early life together and to perhaps shed little more grief out of my system. I knew I still retained some latent feelings of our life together while dating and being engaged to Angela. I felt a few more goodbyes to places we knew and visited might ease my pain even more.

    I made daily trips across town to visit Betty's stepparents, sisters and the cemetery where her mother was buried. I also allowed myself a few side trips down memory lane - to old haunts, houses and places we enjoyed together. Betty's cousin provided me with room and board during my visit.

    The evenings I spent with her and we shared the pains of death and divorce and our future plans. She had recently been separated from her husband and was awaiting a divorce settlement. My sessions in our support group meetings gave me a real appreciation of her difficulties. Coupled with me being widowed, we were on even terms with each other. We had a level of understanding of mutual problems shared by too many people living single in a couple world.

Betty's younger sister looked so much like her I thought they might have been twins. It was a bit scary and I felt unsettled being with her. Betty's half sister had grown into the spitting image of their mother. That was likewise a bit scary and unsettling. I spent enjoyable and informative visits with both of them. So much time had lapsed since Betty's death my trip was more of a social occasion than a part of my grieving.

My daily trek across town passed the federal building where we were married. I recalled the day sentimentally each time how we rode the city bus to our apartment. The grocery store where we bought our wedding day dinner and cake had changed names but it was still in business. These visions in my mind's eye brought out more tears.

We started our married life with little more than the clothes on our backs and a few pieces of personal property. My elation at being married caused me to forget to compensate the judge. His service fee paid for our celebration dinner instead.

Our first residence was in one of two upstairs apartments in a 2 story wood frame house. The living room floor sloped so badly that we had to tie the TV stand to the radiator to keep it from rolling to the center of the room. The kitchen was so quaint a lazy Susan turntable in the middle of the floor would have made it easier to cook and then turn around to do the dishes. Our bedroom was large enough to hold a standard double bed and a very narrow nightstand. You either went in and went to bed or backed out. The bathroom was the only place where we could stretch out without feeling claustrophobic.

It was now 30 years later and as I drove by the old homestead to get a picture for the family photo album, I saw the entire block; including the ranch style brick home of 2400 square feet was gone. An electric substation and a playground had replaced both houses. I felt as though someone had closed the door on my past. I felt cheated out of an important memory and photo.

I left Denver after a week and satisfied I had cleared my calendar of friends and family talks and concluded my residual grieving. I returned to Idaho and to take stock of living with Angela without reservations.

Drinking in a Relationship

It took a short five months of living together to conclude the problem that evaded my reasoning. My trip to Denver wedged the door open. My daily phone calls to the house, to Angela, to check on how things were and how she was getting along were unanswered. She claimed she turned off the phone because of prank calls and telemarketing calls, but actually it was to avoid answering the phone in a drunken stupor. Also it would not waken her while she slept or give her headaches after ringing while she was sobering up.

Angela still retained her drinking problem. Yes, I recognized the symptoms early, but I felt my earlier talks had made a positive influence and that my adoration for her and her feelings for me would help her quit drinking. Instead things got worse. She became more open and even brazen about her drinking the longer we stayed together.

I became more aware there were double meanings behind her catty remarks towards my family and friends, the ones that I had been taking for face value, her true reasons for declining to attend special occasions and social events with me more than once, her reluctance to answer the phone during my absences and her personal injury during my absence one evening.

I had come home one night after a meeting and she was in bed, bleeding, with a cut on her forehead. The gash was still pumping blood as she slept. She blamed the incident on the cat. (He had been locked in the basement.) The physical evidence I examined didn't support her story. Also it kept changing with persistent questioning. She refused medical help. It took my daughter, her boyfriend and two policemen to get her to go to the hospital for medical attention. I was even subjected to looks of being a woman abuser by the police and the hospital staff. If not for my daughter and her boyfriend accompanying me to the hospital that night I may well have been placed under arrest for assault and/or battery.

A month later I went to a convention - alone. Angela refused to accompany me. When I called home she didn't answer the phone. I spent the week at the convention very frustrated.

While there I confided to an associate about my dilemma of living with a possible alcoholic. He himself had been down this road before and I felt he was in a position from experience to advise me on how best to deal with it.

His best advice was not too reassuring. Love, understanding and faith in her ability to want to stop drinking on her own was the single, best, solitary solution. Unless it was her idea there was no hope.

I didn't doubt his advice or his solution but I wanted more, tangible things I could do to promote self-awareness and a cessation of her drinking. He reiterated there wasn't any quick solution. All of it would take time and great deal of effort. I had to submit to time and love. Somehow it didn't seem enough. I knew, I tried repeatedly and I had failed.

But why did I keep trying I kept asking myself? There certainly isn't any instant satisfaction possible in dealing with drinking. My associate's explanation - the person them self must recognize and correct the problem was beyond refute. No form of outside help is any good. If the drinker doesn't want to stop of their own volition they never will. I was devastated!

When I returned home from the convention I found Angela asleep in the spare bedroom. She had undoubtedly been drinking again. I sat down quietly and waited for her to wake up. Four hours later she appeared and was surprised I was home. She had obviously lost track of the days and the time. When I asked what was wrong, she told me she had a headache. She had no reason for sleeping in the wrong room.

My daughter called the next day. We spoke in private. I explained the convention episode to her. She asked me if I had checked on the booze in the house, specifically my miniature bottle collection. I doubted my daughter's question but took faith in her suggestion. What I found was, all the single shot bottles in my collection were empty, including one miniature beer bottle filled with water. I checked the rest of the house, including the cooking sherry, all empty or all gone. My worst fears were realized. Angela had lied about stopping drinking!

The next day being Monday I went to work. My troubled mind wouldn't allow me to concentrate on my tasks. By 9:00 am I got up and went to family support. I pulled every pamphlet on drinking and alcoholism off the shelf and read them all, 19 of them. The one about women and drinking was a slap in the face! I had been a fool! Armed and wide-awake with the knowledge in my hands conveyed to my mind I resolved myself to break our engagement. It took four more days of contemplation but once I was assured she was sober again, I told her our engagement was ended.

Ending the Engagement

We spent a restless and emotional weekend together; Angela begging, pleading and crying not to break up but I didn't give in. She was addicted to drinking from my point of view, plain and simple. She had lied about stopping. She had refused help, including mine, end of discussions.

She spent all day Monday packing her belongings while I was at work. Unable to find anyone else to help her, we spent Tuesday looking at places for her to move in to, another detached apartment or Mother-in-law dwelling as they were called. We spent Wednesday moving her (my son in law helped). I spent Thursday, Friday and Saturday in Sob City as much for me as for her. It was hell for me but eventually I built up enough anger and hate to divorce her from my person. It was the only thing that worked. It took me four months to finally wrench her from my system.

My love for her was sincere however marriage was not a possibility for us nor was staying together. Between our interpersonal family relationships and our philosophical differences and her drinking we parted amicably - fortunately.

I discovered for myself the love I had held for Angela was blind, blinded by emotions, by fears, by loneliness, by desperation. The love I held for Betty never contained those attributes. Neither should another romance if I met another woman and fall in love again. The basis of another relationship would have to find meaning in the same values I held dearest in my marriage to Betty. No more compromises, no more seconds, no more emotional mistakes.

I also discovered or better yet, observed, that a man and a woman, from different families of procreation cannot lie down together and not share troubles as well as happiness. If the relationship is to have any chance of survival, both must accept each other's original families and their members good, bad or indifferent. There's no halfway meeting involved. I nearly drown in a sea of tears and emotions learning this lesson. My engagement ended in part because I forgot that most important fact. Widowed or married the family of your own creation is the most important thing in your life. They exist because of you, not for you. Being in love is not enough to warrant a marriage or form the basis of a long-term relationship. Later, by being alone, I realized I had contributed as much to my daughter's leaving as Angela did.

With the end of our engagement I actually found myself truly alone for the first time since Betty died.

I had now and finally, reached a point in my life where I was without a woman, children and pets. There was no one to leave at home and no one to go home to. I was truly and positively alone for the first time since Betty died. I'd felt better and gotten over it. I'd get through this situation too.

I spent the first two weeks following Angela's departure in depression and deep personal evaluation. (Something I should have accomplished in the sixteen months between Betty's death and becoming engaged to Angela.) In those two weeks I pondered and thought a lot about how I could have better handled the aloneness, which is part of bereavement. My deepest and most thought provoking topic was: It had taken me 21 years to meet and marry Betty; Why should I have expected to meet (and perhaps marry) another woman 21 times faster? The answer to this question was; it would have been best to experience the grief and solitude for at least a traditional full year following the funeral. That year is intended to be the first of many anniversaries of adjustment to living alone not seeking an end to loneliness. Alas, I took a long side trip and suffered greatly for it.

Restructuring My Life

My engagement ended, I took an immediate ten-week leave of absence from work to restructure my personal life and working career. During this period I would take back the life I had almost forsaken, learning to live alone and in solitude, dealing with the effects of widowhood, seeking mental health, examining financial matters in close detail and considering the future of my working career. I had made a gross or better amount of mistakes in the preceding months and it was time to adjust to my environment and cold reality. My suddenly imposed widowhood, seeking other companionship and problems at work had thrust me into chaos. It was time for repose.

The Postpartum Events

I had been without absolute solitude in the 21 months following the death of Betty. I was not unappreciative of the company of another human being, but I was never really left totally alone with my thoughts or to make the mental adjustment to being single. There had always been someone around.

I was with 150 friends and family for a week up until the day of the funeral. It took another week for out of state friends and family to leave. I was saddened by their departures but they had lives and problems of their own to get back to. My adopted mother stayed with me for a week after their departure and then left too in my best interest. And then my youngest daughter, for whom I have the most to thank and the highest admiration, remained at home with Dad while going to school and looking for independence.

I do not begrudge them for staying with me, I only point out that a period of absolute solitude following the death of a spouse is necessary. The shock of physical death is one type to get over. The shock of realizing you are alone and without a personal confidant and companion is another type of death. Both types of shock must be confronted. Aloneness is a learned phenomenon just as living together is learned. It is perhaps a lesson to be learned by being alone.

I spent the first two weeks of my leave scrubbing, washing and polishing the house, the furnishings and the automobiles, using physical labor to work out body tensions by day. As a breather I would spend countless hours in the evenings playing games on the computer and writing. The diversions and the therapy had a positive affect.

My "affair" with Angela had taken a high toll on some of my personal duties. One of the calmer chores I took upon myself during this time was answering cards and letters from Christmas.

I turned my attention to answering the letters from my 1993 Christmas cards. Yes, here it was six months later, past Independence Day and I was writing replies to Christmas letters.

I sent out all my replies and comments to those cards and letters and received but one reply, a letter from a widow back east, Mary, in New England. Our families had met over thirty years ago when we were stationed together for a period of six months in Arkansas. Her husband passed away two years before Betty. The two women had been pen pals. They wrote to each other once or twice a year. Answering her letter seemed a harmless enough task.

The letter in her Christmas card talked about death and widowhood and troubled me deeply. I felt a strong desire to answer it. The events surrounding my life during the beginning of the year had prevented me from answering her immediately. With Angela fairly well out of my mind and no one else left at home to disturb me, I took the time and opportunity to compose a response to her letter. It took nearly eight days of writing, rewriting and editing, then the courage to print and mail the letter, but I did. Little did I realize or anticipate what the future would hold by writing that letter.

To my complete surprise I got an answer back in less than a week. After reading her reply and being pleased at a diversion from housework and an opportunity to be creative, I answered her right back. I went through two revisions later that evening and again in the morning so I could mail it in the afternoon. Again she replied immediately. Five days later I received her reply to my second letter. With subtle semiconscious awareness I began to look forward to her letters. They soon became the most joyous event of my week.

Within a few weeks I became engulfed in writing to Mary and receiving her letters. Without giving much more thought to her than a pen pal status I became totally engrossed in our letter writing. They became the main event of my life and my existence. In a very short time we became pen pals ourselves. I began to live and watch for the mailman every day - even on Sundays.

We set a regular mailing schedule after a few weeks. I would mail a letter to her every Monday unless it was a holiday. The letter should arrive at her home by Thursday or Friday giving her until Monday to formulate and send a reply. And it was damn the post office if the letters were late!

The second half of the year comprises the greater concentration of national holidays and festive occasions-most of which are on Mondays. For us this meant a small problem; mail deliveries would upset our schedule.

To suppress some anxieties I began sending a greeting card on Thursday's so she would have some intermediate contact with me, sort of Hallmark Moment while waiting for my next letter. This arrangement perpetuated itself through December when she called and asked to come west for a visit.

* * *

About the same time I was writing these letters to Mary back east I took to seeing Mamie again. She had been widowed and divorced. She seemed shrouded in the art of being coupled and living single too. She had told me a month after Betty died how she met and married this other fellow and I felt safe being with her in that perspective.

If I she had told me the truth then, that she hadn't really married and her story was just a front to keep uninteresting suitors away, I certainly would have persisted in exploring a more personal relationship with her and lessened, if not avoided, my affair with Angela. I believed Mamie had had an attraction for me even before Betty's death and for some reason unknown to me had decided at this time to be up front and come forward with her feelings.

We had dinner and talked extensively one evening. We revealed our innermost emotions to each other. She began by talking about how she dealt with the death of her son and later her husband. We finally got around to discussing our personal feelings and her story event of nearly two years ago.

She confided how her attraction for me surfaced after being told Betty died and that she had dreamed and fantasized about us periodically ever since. I let her speak for a while then I told her why I went to see her that day in November 1992. I also told her why I left and avoided personal contact thereafter. She told me she was sick at having told me that story. It was in bad taste and sorely out of context, but I looked as if I'd lost my best friend and she hoped to cheer me up. She was half correct. Her abdominal pains were so intense at my leaving she couldn't get her feet to follow after me and tell me the story was a lie.

With all my feelings out in the open I felt cleansed and relieved. I told her if had I known she was not really married before I met Angela I would have chased her to the end of the world. We made some agreements that evening. We agreed to continue to see each other for as often as circumstances permitted, to maintain a platonic relationship we could both break away from if an end time came or pursue further should it become possible and to maintain as best as possible a camaraderie type of relationship. The understanding I hoped to achieve materialized.

I felt a great inner peace with myself knowing I could continue to write Mary and maintain a rapport with Mamie and have neither contact interfere with the other.

It is against my nature, although I tried a few times, to participate in more than one relationship at a time. As I illustrated earlier, the time I dated more than one woman in a week, I was screwed up mentally for nearly a month afterwards. I felt in this instance however I could keep both women separated physically and mentally while I sorted out my contacts with them.

I became confused with myself again. I seemed to be looking at one woman after another. But what was I in search of? Romance, companionship, love, marriage, an affair, what????? I found it alarming that the women who braved to know me, have dates with me once or twice, became attracted to me. What was it an old Air Force buddy told me one day? Just be yourself around women. The more I was, the more romantically involved I become with them and not always with the best of intentions from either of us. What was the solution?

To this end I would later discover and order, a book titled, "*Making Love Happen*" by Rebecca Sydnor. If dating again was going to be possible then the cautious words of advice from someone in success was necessary.

Embracing Singleness

Nearly two years passed since the funeral. I'd gone through all the ups and downs associated with widowhood, death itself, a family gathering, the firsts of special occasions alone, holidays, anniversaries, birthdays and places and events meant for two people. A family at odds with me and itself, a well-intentioned engagement and break up and now finally, truly, living alone and in solitude. It wasn't a bad place, not one I'd recommend for myself to live, but a short visit was valuable. At last I was dealing with loneliness and absolute solitude for the first time. I hated to admit it, but the event for me was long overdue.

Living alone was not as bad as I thought it might be. However, I was now committed to living alone for a while, not because I wanted to, but because I had to. I had to find out who I am, who I was and the all-important question; "What do I want to do now that I am alone and maintain that livelihood for the next 12 months?" Leaving women alone, workshop projects and recreational therapy surfaced as my solutions.

I'd allowed a great deal of chores and improvements to go unattended. It was perhaps the best time and thing for me to dive headlong into a life of solitude and housework and home improvements. A year of isolation from a social life should be sufficient towards that end. How did I feel? Better than nothing, better than most.

I set about using physical labor first to work out the tensions and frustrations I was feeling. The house could use another through cleaning spring and fall. Angela was not a bad housekeeper, quite the opposite, however portions of the heavier cleaning were beyond her physical abilities. It was to these chores I set my mind and body.

The five weeks following our break up were spent in near absolute solitude. My primary attentions were devoted to cleaning, home repair and improvements and writing. These activities were upset occasionally when Angela stopped by or phoned for a "What went wrong?" discussion making the adjustment more difficult for me. Part of my problem in separating myself from Angela became my occasional and cautious visits to her apartment after our break up. But aside from those visits, no other visitors, no friends, no family, just me and the house and my thoughts.

I supposed the both of us were still looking for the answers to our break up, she more intently than me. Perhaps sobriety and reality had finally set in. I was unsure. I was positive of one thing, I couldn't trust her or her motives no matter how sincere they might have sounded. (I sensed an element of deja vue from our initial meetings months before in our kiss and make up meetings.) I restated to her and to myself, the engagement was over. We tried, it didn't work and so what was the use in perpetuating it? I could only conclude she would rather be miserable with a bottle than happy with me.

After those five weeks of being alone it became easier. I was for the most part gratified. Our separation however would prove no easier than bereavement.

* * *

My mental condition following the end of my engagement sent me to a mental health clinic of my own free choice. There I discussed in sordid detail the events of my widowhood, engagement and my job troubles with a psychiatrist. It took eight weeks of thinking out loud to him to bring about my self-assurance of future financial security and renewed emotional confidence of what changes in my life were both necessary and desirable.

The doctor himself never made any outright recommendations, he only asked pertinent questions, those I would not allow myself to ask of me. From those one sided discussions I made a conscious decision to restructure my finances, to quit work altogether, stay home alone and become a house-husband to myself, to rejoin my family together and most importantly - allow myself 12 months of unencumbered living - alone.

* * *

The last six months of 1993 I concentrated on home repair and improvement therapy when not writing letters. After cleaning they helped to further work out the physical strains built up in my body from my engagement and my decisions. I managed to complete a few minor home improvement projects in those few months. Among them were replacing the curtain rods and curtains in five rooms, installing valances in the bedrooms, ceiling tile in the basement; I repaired, restored and sold furniture, reversed the iron gate swing between the house and garage and repainted my daughter's former bedroom. I did a fair amount by myself, however I was not immune to asking for some help from my son-in-law when conditions warranted.

I also had a yard sale and got rid of some memorabilia, household goods and auction junk I no longer needed.

Resigning From Work

I had long pondered and discussed the possibilities of another retirement with other workers. My job position looked unstable for the future. There were always ongoing management cutbacks of personnel and budget restraints. So I sat down for the second time in my life and considered real change - change similar to selling out and moving but not quite that drastic.

At the end of my ten-week leave of absence I returned to my work place to see my supervisor. He was not pleased, nor happy with my decision to resign but after an extensive discussion he did finally understand the depth and breadth of my reasons and my needs. He reluctantly consented to accepting my paperwork. We made immediate arrangements for transfer of my workload to other technicians and engineers.

Within a week I was gone from the stresses imposed by my job. I left work that day with the same feeling as concluding a successful shopping trip at a grocery store.

Yes, I resigned my job with the Federal Service. The stresses in working had become more than I could bear, coupled with my personal and private problems and a few trips to mental health, it became painfully obvious those serious and permanent changes had been in order. I made some difficult but necessary decisions and then put them into action. I was better off now and I knew it. I made conditional plans to enter self-employment with my workshop and/or taking part time employment in nonmanagement jobs later if the opportunity presented itself. If not, I would be financially stable for two years, or more, of unencumbered life alone.

Romance by Rebecca/Other Relationships

Three months after I broke my engagement with Angela I bought a book titled "*Making Love Happen*." Not the sort of book a man would be expected to read but the synopsis had appeal. In reading it I became painfully aware of the transgressions I had made in dating and cultivating my previous relationships.

I made a self-examination of my errors in dealing with dating and courting so soon after Betty's death and another examination of the differences between divorced and widowed women.

My affair with Angela behind me I began to ponder if I shouldn't have looked closer at more of the (widowed) friends of Betty instead. In them, I could have found someone much more akin to my feelings, education, experience and understanding. The world of divorced women for me had been disastrous. Perhaps the world of widows would have held better promise.

In my new grief I decided to look around, at a distance, at which of Betty's friends were radiant with her and widowed and still single. There were some ladies in particular I thought might make a good companion for me if they were still available. Quite frankly I didn't know. I would have to see them and talk to them. I had a year to contemplate and Rebecca's book as a guide.

I turned my attention to focusing on the personal points of view that I ignored before in my pursuit of happiness and to wash away the grief I was feeling. I had a need to know what had broken and to make a plan to prevent it from happening again should I chose to become involved with yet another woman after my year of self imposed solitude.

Among the more passive chapters I observed that while I was looking for a custom built Cadillac style woman, I had been settling for stock model Chevrolet's. Therein lay my problem. I made up a nonnegotiable list as called for in her book. I started with 30 or more undesirable qualities and 20 or so desirable qualities. In the end I resigned myself to five really important issues, drinking, smoking gambling, children and most of all, family. I crossed off the rest as trivial to a second or successive companion. I was not dating, courting, or even marrying second best.

In reading this particular book I found it to be too much like a textbook in form. This I felt was a little self-defeating. I was looking for simplified answers to simplified questions in prose not a lesson in social etiquette in text type instruction. A narrative prose explaining purposeful dating with sound reasoning was my goal. I did find some prose in this book but it still offered romance and love more as a business proposition than the sought after emotional satisfactions.

The book achieved its goal with me albeit too formal. The chapter on desirable qualities and the chapter on undesirable qualities made the most significant impact. I applied them prudently and succeeded in finding another lifelong companion. A Jimmy Hatlo Tip of the Hat to you Rebecca.

As a result of reading her book again and again, I set for myself five steadfast rules by which my next romantic encounter must abide, no excuses, no compromises.

My recent affair with Angela had illuminated a real bright light, family. My family was my most important asset. It was because of me they existed. They were my responsibility. The noun family meant help for no other reason than they were family. The same rule would apply in a successive relationship for me. Hence, I made my one and only positive rule, first families first. My immediate family came first to me in my dealings with them. The same must hold true for another woman, whomever she may be. I held tight to the thought: In each life some rain must fall. You can't sleep with another woman and not expect to get wet too. Whenever rain falls in either forest, both of you will be impacted by the dampness. Also, whatever either of us acquired before our marriage would remain the inheritance of the first family.

I made up a list of four negative rules to abide by. Top of the list; No drinking, simple enough, drinking is a disease. I do not and cannot drink. My health won't allow it. My previous engagement elevated this rule to the top of the "no" list. I had shielded myself from the harmful effects of drinking for so long I had forgotten all the pitfalls that lay before and around me. I became blind, even oblivious, to the damnable events that can occur living with a person who chooses to drink regardless of the reason or the amount.

Next, no smoking, simple enough too. Smoking is also a disease and an addiction. I don't smoke and with my history of lung ailments I no longer do. Betty smoked until she died. She wouldn't stop smoking after watching me gain weight after I quit. (The reason for my weight gain was because my body resumed growth after I quit smoking. The doctor's observation - not mine.) She lived in mortal fear of obesity. She wound up full figured for a while during her child bearing that lasted ten years. She began losing weight significantly after arriving in Idaho. She almost had her waistline back when she died. Also, the newest reports of second hand smoke lended themselves to creditability.

Next, no gambling, simple enough also. Gambling is also a disease. Even innocent people tend to over indulge. I look around at the proprietors of gambling establishments and I'm offended at how much wealth they acquired without lifting a finger. Their patrons are a captivated audience seeking a thrill and willing to use money as the source of their excitement. My own rule is I gamble as much as I can afford to loose, which is nothing. I do not intend to contribute to another person's flamboyant life-style.

Between rules 1, 2, & 3 I had saved enough money to own a car and truck and house. A horrendous thought.

The last negative rule I made was no children new or otherwise. I was certainly too old and impoverished to start a new family. I could barely afford to raise my own children in my prime. I couldn't begin to calculate the cost of raising a second family in conjunction with having grandchildren. I didn't want or need the burden of continuing child rearing into and beyond my golden years. As to children otherwise, I was not raising children, mine or another woman's, until I die. Children and grandchildren are welcome to visit and that is all. I was not inclined to raise my children and their children into my grave.

I gave up my best (physical) years to sire and raise my children. I had raised them the best way I knew. Now it was up to them to show me I raised them correctly by going out into the world and showing me they can make it with the education, experience and love they were given, without having to live at or return home in my golden years.

I figure each person is entitled to three childhood's, their grandparents, their parents and their own. Most people would think I have it backwards. I don't think so. I was a child to my grandparents. I was a child to my parents. And in this stage of life I am my own child. I spent 20 years being a child to my parents. I spent another 30 years raising my children. Now I want to be the child at an age when I can live it and enjoy it.

* * *

My dating again, or meetings with other women to be more to the point, was a failed attempt. I did date and see more divorcees and widows and even significant other types of women during my solitude, all to no avail. Their company was good and we enjoyed each other's presence but it was unfulfilling. What was lacking was commitment. Either there wasn't any or it wasn't possible.

My list from Rebecca was self-eliminating. I was still seeing women with new families in mind, women who drank, women who smoked, women who gambled and worst of all, still had children at home, in ages that ranged from 10 years to 49 years. My needs of a second helpmate excluded all these circumstances.

After four months of dating, August through November 1994, two real possibilities of companionship came before me, both widows, Mamie and Mary. Both offered me the best solutions to my list. Who would be best? Who was most sincere? Who needs who more?

It was at this point I recalled that when I was attending the support group there was a session wherein the group topic was "Personal Ads." Later, after the group session ended I returned to work to ponder, and once back home "drafted" a personal ad. I looked for and found the original ad. I amended and expanded on those initial qualities - satirically.

This was what I came up with:

Widowed White Male, Semi retired

Who wants an old fart of 50 years, 6'2", 185 lbs (paunchy but not fat), balding, brown/gray hair (what's left of it), fair health with a history of hypertension, emphysema, hemorrhoids, muscle cramps, hiatal hernia, chest pains, costochondrasitis, gout, bad dentition, halitosis and no prize for good habits; non-drinker (obviously), nonsmoker (obviously), no kids (new or otherwise), no pets (including everything from snakes with no legs to centipedes with one hundred legs) and no gambling, (living on a fixed income). Dabbles in wood crafting (makes copious amounts of composting materials), enjoys yard sales (for exercise), auctions (for entertainment) and western events (for outdoor activities), VHS videos (of my own collection), movies (on Tightwad Tuesdays), music (below 80 decibels), fireside dinners (not Banquet or Swanson); leads a quiet, sedate and subdued lifestyle; is kind, considerate and gentle; reads, writes and talks (sometimes too much); and goes fishing once every 29 years. Is interested in a woman with a great deal of courage and compassion to tolerate these qualities. Reply in person. Serious inquires only.

For what I considered editorial reasons I shared it with Mamie and Mary. To my chagrin, both said yes, in particular, Mary. I was surprised and flattered. (I would discover later that Mary's husband and I shared most of these attributes.)

Chapter 10

The Recovery of My Consciousness

"I know what is in my head.
I know what is in my heart.
I do not know what is in the heavens."

Restructuring My Personal Life

After reading and rereading books about love and marriage and death and divorce and their impact on love the second (or successive) time around I chose by preference to reexamine this world of the widows more closely. Women wrote all the books available on the market. There were none I could find written by men, for men, for me a tremendous vacuum. I knew what was in my head. I knew what was in my heart. I didn't have a clue what was in the heavens for me. My meetings with Mamie kept her in my head and on my mind nearly exclusively. Physical contact and ease of access seemed to thrust us together. My letters to Mary kept her closer to my heart and my soul. A rapport developed through writing to each other that brought us closer together through what I refer to as psychic awareness. Whatever the heavens held in store for me between them was totally elusive.

Divorced Versus Widowed Women

My own impression of the divorced women I met and dated was that most of them were bitter but not all. These women had been dumped by their husbands or had dumped them.

It was apparent to me there was a level of expectation in divorcees in which one or the other partner had not been ready, willing or able to deal with. Some of these problems were insignificant (irreconcilable differences), while others were more intense (adultery).

There is an exception to every rule and in my case the one divorcee I thought might make a good wife was really too secretive for me.

I had shunted the idea of dating widows for fear of competing with a dead person. The same ideology exists with divorced women but their ex's are still out there, still walking the streets.

Divorce in a relationship is similar to untying the waist strings of an apron and letting it dangle from the neck whereas death in relationship is similar to removing the apron entirely.

I sought solace in my decision to examine the world of widows more closely. Someone with something in common with me and in real terms wanted to put the past behind her and get on with living again.

Meeting Mary

My self-imposed solitude lasted six months. Yes, I had "dated" during this period, but no overnight visits or continuous dating. Also, in the intervening period, I had become pen pals with the widow Mary in New England. I had sent her family newsletters for the last three Christmas seasons and on this latest occasion she responded.

I had put off answering her sooner because I was engaged early in the year and felt a reply might be presumptuous. My engagement broken, the presumptions ended and needing a respite from the tedious affairs of solitude I set about writing letters to people who had taken the time to answer my newsletter. Her letter was one of those. (Writing these letters would also become part of the reunification of my family and friends.)

I had been troubled by the content of her last letter and her comments about death in general. It seemed to me, on the surface, she had never really gotten the grieving out of her system. She had experienced multiple deaths between 1988 and 1992, Her mother, husband and now a close personal pen pal. The grief she was experiencing was coming too fast and frequent for her to expel.

I wrote and asked if she needed a confidante to share her misery with. Initially she was offended, however, in time she became less offended and more receptive to discussion by mail. We corresponded steadily for the first six months of my self-imposed solitude.

Then, early one day in December she called and asked me what I was doing for the holidays? "Nothing," was my reply, "sharing it with friends if any stopped by, but nothing specific or purposeful."

She invited herself to visit Idaho and me. I was stunned at her suggestion and numbly agreed to the visit.

After our conversation it dawned on me to what I had consented to, a full week with a widow - alone! What was I to do? Well for one, I needed to keep us both busy. No use leaving the door open to moral interpretation. Frankly, I was scared and my intention of living year in solitude was being upset. Now a week alone, with a widowed woman? Oh well, I thought to myself. It's too late to back out now. Be the perfect host and play everything by ear.

I must admit it was a glorious and wonderful week. I met her at the airport sporting flowers and a balloon blazoned with "X's" and "O's," a symbol of our letter sign off's in recent weeks. Parallel to most wedding rituals nothing started right. Her connection in Cincinnati was delayed by an aircraft navigation system failure. Her connection in Salt Lake City was missed and she was bumped to another flight. I sat in the airport lobby looking every bit the languid lover with most of the toddlers in the terminal gleaming at my balloon. Two toddlers even asked for it. She arrived two flights late and very tired. Both the flowers and the balloon lightened her mental fatigue.

Her first question was could she have a cup of coffee. She hadn't had much time between flights for a restful cup. We left the gate and headed for the coffee shop. There we chatted and drank coffee while waiting for her luggage. I saw a sparkle in her eyes I hadn't seen in 30 years.

After all the other passengers got their bags and no more luggage was forthcoming from the conveyor belt we reported to lost baggage claim. The attendant informed us the luggage missed the connecting flights and wouldn't arrive for another hour. If we would leave my address, the airline would deliver the luggage directly to my home by midnight. We agreed to let the airline handle the problem. We spent the interlude between her luggage arrival and bedtime watching "Sleepless in Seattle" and recalling bygone days. Her luggage arrived shortly after the movie ended. She had nightclothes and we could retire.

The visit was over scheduled for things to do. Travel wise I would show her the Perrine Bridge at Twin Falls and the view of the city golf course beneath the bridge and beside the Snake River, to a mineral hot springs near Hagerman, a diner in Bliss that served buffalo burgers, a tour of the local air base, to our veteran charity bingo, a local auction, a cheese factory tour, a picnic and to see the Halley, Ketchum and Sun Valley mountain resorts. New Year's Eve meant a fireside dinner at my home and watching the red apple descend in Times Square at midnight. On New Year's Day we would watch the Rose Parade from Pasadena via satellite and in an interlude she would meet my family members residing in Idaho before returning home.

The next day we went to Twin Falls, the other big city near my home. I showed her the suspension bridge over the Snake River and pointed out the municipal golf course on the river's edge. (A tale to tell her golfing brother.) Next I kept my promise of a hot bath, a heated swimming pool and mineral spring in Hagerman. After the hot pool we dined at the buffalo burger bar in Bliss. She opted for the normal beef type. From there we went for a nickel tour of the Air Base. She hadn't seen an active military base in ten years. Then it was home to dinner and onto bingo where I was scheduled to work, a voluntary and community deed. I bought a stack of cards for her to play, for me while I worked, and to give her some social entertainment. She blended with the crowd as if she'd been coming here for years.

The next day we went to a public auction in Boise. I bought very little. I stayed close to her all day, my arms wrapped around her waist, kissing her hair occasionally. After the auction we went to the cheese factory. I wanted sweet butter. Alas, early shoppers had cleared out the factory cases. The factory restaurant had already closed for the day. The plant was in the process of being cleaned and the workers were getting ready for the long New Year's weekend. We settled for some cheese samplers and went home.

Mary suggested a homemade dinner for the evening and I agreed. Boy, was I surprised when she pulled a recipe book out of her suitcase and asked me to choose a preference of four meals! (She's the only woman I met who packs a recipe book when she travels.) While she prepared my dinner selection I started a fire and we moved the dining table to the living room to eat by the fireplace.

After dinner we played cards until the ball fell over Times Square marking 1995 - in New York! She had forgotten about the time zone differences. We wished one another a happy New Year and I told her that custom established that the first person you kiss in the New Year would be the person you spend most of the New Year with. From where I was I couldn't think of a better person to be with. I kissed her that evening under the mistletoe. I guess it was then I came to realize I was very attracted to her.

For the next two hours we spoke of idyllic inclinations. Small talk mostly. The stuff two people attracted to one another would enjoy. Two hours later when midnight crossed our time zone I repeated my earlier statements and added, "I think I love you." Perhaps it was Andy Williams' rendition of a song by the same title that popped into my head, I don't know but Mary mimicked my words. We kissed passionately and spoke softly of rekindled feelings.

New Years Day morning was breakfast by the fireside, a Sunday paper and more subtle talk of a possible life together. She was wanting, but unwilling to commit. She wanted to sort out her feelings first. She hadn't used them in four years. She told me she didn't come to Idaho to become romantically involved. She came out to slow me down, to make me think - out load if necessary, about my life and myself. My letters had become too inviting, too muddled and too involved.

Dinner was light followed by the movie, "*A River Runs Through It.*" Halfway through she fell asleep in my arms. I felt comfortable and she was peaceful lying there. After the movie ended I woke her up and we retired properly for the evening.

The next day we went to Hailey, Ketchum and Sun Valley to see the mountains and ski resorts. Except for a blown muffler it was a quiet and serene trip.

Later in the day she became ill from the (common) cold she brought with her. I bundled her up, gave her medication and made her rest. I kept watch over her while she slept. The following morning I woke up, sick as a puppy myself. Had I caught her cold or was mine an allergy attack? At any rate, we exchanged places and I took a turn on the couch to recover.

My kids and grandkids came over that night. I sat out the evening with the chills while the three of them played cards for a few hours. My daughter and her family went home early. Mary had an early flight in the morning and I needed more rest to chauffeur her.

My fever broke about 2:00 am. By 5:00 am I was okay. Before we left the house I told Mary that no matter what decision she made about us and a possible life together the feelings I'd developed for her were not going to change.

Most of our discussions had been about family and friends, philosophies, values and bridging the gap of the last 31 years. Falling in love and proposing during the visit was not on my agenda. She declined me an immediate answer to my feelings and my proposal. She wanted time to think.

The decisions she had to make included giving up her job, losing her retirement and her family's closeness; going from independent to dependent; moving; what to do between interludes; what to do with her house, the impact on her children, grandchildren and other relatives; getting another job here if she decides to work and remarriage. Was she willing to start over? Was I worth it?

I drove her to the airport, said my good-byes, told her again I loved her and asked her why she didn't say so again after midnight on New Year's. She told me when she said it again she would be sure she really meant it and wasn't giving in to the romance of the moment. I stayed until her plane taxied to the runway. She went back to her world and I was left alone again in mine.

I was shattered at her departure when her visit ended. The last time I felt so alone and hopeless was when my kids went home after the funeral. The revelations and the feelings were very unsettling in their similarities. Why did

I propose to her on a first meeting? "Because," as she would relate later, "it felt so right."

I had fallen in love with her. Not by design, just fell in love. I became captivated by her aura, her personae.

What a whirlwind visit!

* * *

I continued to date and seeing other women (Mamie in particular) after Mary left but my heart wasn't in it. I missed her companionship and her personality too badly. We had an established rapport built up by corresponding with each other through our weekly letters and greeting cards and now coupled with her visit I felt lost again in a couple world.

After two months of separation she wrote and asked to visit me again, this time on a return trip from a tournament she had planned to attend. I consented with all the flavors a child going to the local ice cream parlor for a treat would have. She said she would bring with her the answer to my proposal.

Dating Mamie

The widow I'd known for some time, Mamie, confronted me also in early December with an invitation to call her the next day, which I did. As we talked I got the impression she was attracted to me. (A delayed reaction from our previous meetings.) I believed the attraction and its basis formed through our casual visits and conversations before and after my hospital appointments. She also divulged to me her relationship with the man I thought was her husband and who was really just a significant other was on the skids. I told her about Mary's impending visit.

We made a date to meet at a restaurant for brunch after Mary left. There, she quizzed me about how the visit went with the lady from the east. I told her it all went well, keeping my answers broad and somewhat vague. At my answers she resembled an inflated balloon going flat. I don't know why but I felt like I had made her happy and relieved. (I did not reveal to her I had proposed to Mary.)

She spoke briefly of her discontent with her significant other. She felt the relationship went astray after the first six months and hadn't improved since. I recounted with similar tales of my own, specifically with Angela whom I almost married. Still, I felt Mamie had more on her mind and that more might be me.

I talked for a while and she talked for a while. Finally, she suggested a trip to Jackpot, Nevada sometime soon. I opposed the idea based on the distance and my concepts about gambling. I really felt the suggestion to be something of a ruse. And I was right in a sense. When she countered her own suggestion that we really didn't have to go to Jackpot that we could just sit and talk at my place it would be okay too. At this point I became certain Mamie held feelings for me. How sincere they were remained for her to say, clearly and distinctly but at another time and place.

We finished our coffee and parted. She left to go to work. I half promised to see her again later, at her office, after completing some errands and dinner too if she felt like it.

I was left in the diner confused and musing. I now felt certain Mamie held loving feelings for me. How sincere they were remained for her to say. I also became more assured Mamie had had an attraction for me for some time and at an odd time, today, chose to be up front and forward with it.

I decided to meet with Mamie again later in the afternoon, have dinner with her and talk more about our respective feelings, with others as well as each other. I also felt if I didn't have this nurturing relationship with Mary developing I might go ahead and try to cultivate more than a platonic relationship with her.

I felt a compulsion to meet with Mamie, lay all my feelings and prospects upon the table and see what goes where and when. I could confess I felt an attraction for her two years ago but I felt stronger about seeing my new relationship with Mary to a definite conclusion first. I did not believe for a moment Mary would ask an end to our relationship, but if she did, I felt I wanted the door to the relationship with Mamie to remain open. Could I expect her to wait up to a year to get an answer?

* * *

My musings over both women drove me to comparing them with each other.

On the Atlantic side of the continent was Mary, a lovely woman, healthy, happy and eager to stop being lonely. She was the marrying kind, a down to earth motherly woman whose primary interests were family and friends. Her interests paralleled my own. A marriage to her would not cause either of us financial problems. There would of course be hurdles to overcome if such a marriage were to take place.

On the Pacific side of the continent was Mamie, also a lovely woman, healthy and happy but seemingly lonely? Once widowed and once divorced and now living with a significant other, she did not seem to be the marriageable kind. She was not nearly as motherly a woman and her primary interests were family and friends. Her interests also paralleled my own, however, her philosophies and methods of attaining them were unusual to me. A marriage wouldn't really be necessary to be happy with her. For her to remarry she would lose most of her income permanently.

* * *

From January through September 1995 I maintained my weekly letters and cards to Mary. Here at home I drifted into an equally regular activity of meeting Mamie for dinner and conversation. Mentally it wasn't easy keeping both women separated, from inside of me as well as from each other. Physically, Mary was at a disadvantage. The sense of touch is a powerful aphrodisiac.

My meetings with Mamie centered more on what we came to call, "The doctor is in" talks. More often than not they became muddled in romantic inclinations by both of us. At first we seemed to be thrust into meeting each other. Later, after three months of frequent meetings, events cooled and we seemed to be kept separated for one odd reason or another - by fate or destiny.

She would propose meetings and cancel them later, most times at the last minute or within hours of our agreed time. For me, the incidents became contemptible. I had been brought up in an atmosphere of courtesy and consideration. As our relationship continued broken dates became more frequent and a barrier between us before we would revert back to our original friendship status.

It had some outside help and outside influences. For as much as we seemed thrust together initially, the later half of our intended, "Is the doctor in?" talks were seemingly prevented by third party and third event intervention wedges. Perhaps it was my intension to homebody Mamie or my reluctance to join her on compulsive trips to far away places in the middle of the night for fun and food. I began to sense a haunting, a desire by her to return to a relationship comparable to the one that existed with her deceased husband. I felt no need or desire to follow a dead man's footpath. Or, just perhaps, it was the trip to New England I planned after Labor Day.

By September our relationship reverted back to a distant friend status. This did coincide with my scheduled trip to New England and meeting Mary in her world, her friends and family.

* * *

By all previous accounts I had wandered into another dichotomy, in particular, the name thing again. I was courting two women simultaneously. Mary ending in "y" only and Mamie ending in "ie." Before me lay another pair of women whose names followed in my observations of my past encounters. Angela had maintained the status quo picture of the "a" ending. What was I to learn from this present adventure?

The name game would continue.

Chapter 11

A New Awakening

"Touch the right man for the right reason, be it as a friend, as a lover, or as a husband."

Setting Better Standards

Several women had touched me in the last two years, some trying to be friendly, some looking for a lover and still others looking for a husband. They knew, or thought they knew, what they were looking for in a companion. I, on the other hand, didn't know who or what or why I was really looking at other women. When my affair with Angela ended, I sat down to take a stern look at what it was I wanted, or better yet - needed, in a woman. I resolved myself to two solutions, 1) a year in solitude and 2) to set some better standards. I felt a year of self imposed solitude would give me ample time to make all the necessary changes required of me to establish a continued life of solitude or make room for another woman. It would also give me ample time to review my needs from another woman, what they should be and to use them to begin a search for her.

Meeting Mary Again

Mary called me again in February to ask about a second visit in April. The nature of her call was to find out if it was okay. She would be attending a tournament in Arizona and the side trip back through Boise would only cost $50.00 more than a direct return. She had considered long and hard the two proposals I had made to her in December. My formal proposal of marriage and an informal question that I had proposed, "Could she live here, in Idaho, in this house, with me?" The question as I had offered it was to determine for myself if we were to have a life together would it be here in Idaho or in Massachusetts or somewhere else? She would bring both answers with her. I consented gleefully.

Her personae gave no hint as to her answers to my proposals. She was the kind of woman who would spend the time and the effort, in person, to say "no" as well as "yes" to my proposals. She believed in face-to-face meetings over "Dear John" letters and phone calls. The twelve weeks of waiting felt more like twelve months to me. The anxiety and anticipation were nearly unbearable. For this occasion and visit I made no plans. Whatever she wanted to do was fine by me. If that meant more talking and less travel, so be it. And as such it was.

We spent the four days and nights talking a great deal. When we were both satisfied camaraderie had developed and a companionship was possible I gave in again to my feelings and formally proposed again, this time with less loneliness/emotional involvement. She stated she wanted to, however there were obstacles, her family, friends and lifestyle. To resolve them, we concluded a meeting with her family and friends was in order and a trip to New England by me was essential to a continuing relationship. We made plans for me to visit in September.

* * *

In my mind's eye I felt better about this proposal with Mary than with any other women I asked or contemplated asking. The reason was I sat down and made out a "score card" of sorts for all the women I had dated and a few others I had contemplated about. I ruled out drinking as number one, followed by smoking, gambling and children still at home as negative prospects. The sole positive aspect and to me the most important, was first families first. It was this topic more than the remaining four on which I placed my highest hopes. Another woman in my life had to consider her own family more important to her than even me. This condition must be reciprocal and respected by both of us.

These points may take on a business tone in a relationship, but it is essential to the mental health of merging two families of different origins. As your lives are shared, so are your families. It is hoped and fervently, both families will get along after meeting each other. It is a risk all widows and widowers, as well as divorcees must take. It is up to both new partners in a new relationship to be willing to accept the other person's family differences, in upbringing, attitudes and principles.

Mary had met my family and had been accepted warmly and wholeheartedly. My trip to New England should achieve a similar result. By my own observations we both maintained a lot of the same principles in our own separate families. This I felt would save the day and the visit.

Visiting New England

My visit to New England was everything I hoped it would be. From being with Mary again to satisfying a life long aspiration of seeing New England. I arrived by plane on a Friday night. From the airport we went to dinner then to her home where I met her youngest daughter and granddaughter who were living with her. Mary showed me her home as I had shown her mine. A sort of adult level joke between us, you show me yours, I show you mine type of humor.

She was the tour director on this visit. Her plans for the two-week visit would begin tomorrow. Saturday would be errand day, the usual breakfast at the local donut Shoppe followed by a quiet afternoon. On Sunday I would be the "guest of honor" and meet all of her family, daughters, son-in-laws and grandchildren. Thereafter, we were scheduled to attend the states fair for a day; spend part of a day at her office meeting her boss and co-workers, three days and nights in Vermont visiting more of her relatives, touring Northwestern New Hampshire and taking a loop drive through Canada. We were offered four days and nights on Cape Cod at her boss' pleasure, a summer retreat which would include joining up with more of her friends on a two week retreat of their own, a tour of Cape Cod following the trails blazed by the pilgrims first arrival in America to the witches trials in Salem; and to dine in the Colony Club at the expense and desires of her daughters before my departure the following morning.

* * *

"Are you ready to go to breakfast?" Mary asked me.

"Yes," I said.

This Saturday morning and today was the beginning of my introduction into her life-style. I had arrived by plane late in the afternoon yesterday. She met me at the airport in gleeful anticipation. After we collected my baggage and had taken it out to the car she revealed her plans for dinner. Plan "A" was an all-you-can-eat salad bar on the way home. Plan "B" was a steak house west of town.

The traffic was a mess at the exit to the Plan "A" dinner spot from the interstate so we opted for the Plan "B" choice.

The steak house was an old barn converted to a restaurant. We dined in simple pleasure up in the loft near a window from which we could see the pasture of the farm below and the sunset over the meadow beyond. She ordered steak, which I did not care about. For me she suggested a local fish entrée, baked scrod. The suggestion was appealing and in keeping with our generations etiquette, she was paying and both were of near equal prices, I consented to try it. The meal was Astoria Hotel quality in its simple way.

In the standards of older, established, New England customs we spent nearly two hours dining. I had long understood New England life was laid back, reposed and for the most part unhurried. Aside from still feeling jet lag by flying (nearly) coast to coast, I had a yearning and a longing for a slower paced life-style. I had moved to the great northwest over five years before to get away from the rigors and rat race of life in California. I felt I was more than ready for another, slower pace of living, if such a thing was possible. We chatted idyllically about our plans for the next two weeks, daily routines, special events, tourist spots and meeting her family and friends.

This morning came and we started our trek, first to the post office then to the liquor store for lottery tickets and now to the donut Shoppe.

The shop was quaint and unique to say the least. It was situated at the end of a line of small shops. The inside of the shop was similar in many contrasts to donut shops across the country, a line of booths, a line of tables and a counter. The walls were decorated with county life paraphernalia; old pie servers, a seven slice pie cutter, ice cream scoops, bread basket, cutting boards, dried flowers, kitchen utensils, animal silhouettes, carriage lanterns, an Easter Bonnet, a pendulum clock framed by a cut out of a country house and homey welcoming signs like "All ye who enter here must wear a smile." and "Sit long - talk much." None of the heralded atmosphere associated with the major fast food chains, stiff preformed uncomfortable booths, small tables and chairs, backless counter stools, or bland walls covered with sterile photographs, those reminiscent of fast food turnover by a "keep the customers changing" atmosphere. Here we were, surrounded by family, friends and neighbors, very few strangers in the midst.

The shop for me held a most unique and thought provoking concept. The walls and overhangs behind the counter were filled with coffee cups and mugs of every size and description made possible by human imagination. In addition to the walls and overhangs in the far corner adjacent to the donut counter was a bulletin board style and arrangement of cups. The plaque inside the squared arrangement of 12 cups read, "Sunday Morning Bike Boys." *Now here's a real diversion from the old established tradition of look alike coffee cups in virtually every donut shop I'd been in before* I thought to myself. There was one exception that came to my mind. The donut shop in my home town served coffee in the same mug to each customer except the customers placed their own names or "brands" on the cups to differentiate one customer's mug from another. I say "brands" because life in the northwest is western style and more aptly describes the scribbles on the cups without actual names. And, in my hometown, the cups were hung on the wall in the customer area where they were returned after each use.

Normally she sat at the counter with her other single friends, but this morning she opted for the semi-privacy of a booth, the one in the corner of the shop. I could feel a physic air of, "So this is the new guy we haven't heard too much about or seen before now," permeating the air by the other customers as we walked to the booth.

We ordered breakfast and coffee. As we waited, she began to "introduce" me quietly to the other customers present around the donut shop. The introductions were her descriptions of the various people seated around the donut shop this particular morning and time of day. She told me of their professions and their relationships.

She began by describing the people in the booths, starting with the couple seated directly in front of us and moving slowly away to the farthest booth then to the far end of the counter working her way around it, back towards the line of tables, through the line of tables and finally back to us. By the end of her tour I had "met" a fair cross representation of the local community, each of who could tell his or her own story of their lives, good or bad.

I have no doubt their lives contained as many ups and downs as the roads in town contained frost heaves and potholes. Still, when she was done, I felt a part of the town within me, and a part of belonging to it, not just her.

When the waitress brought us our coffee I noticed hers was cup from the wall but mine was in a standard white cup and saucer indicative of franchise restaurants. I was a little dismayed. On her cup was printed "To Mother With Love." Mine was sterile and white and devoid of identity. I felt as transparent as the finish on the cup. I asked my fiancée why the mug for her and the cup and saucer for me? She explained it to me this way. "The cups and mugs on the walls and overhangs belong to specific customers. They were given to customers by the previous owners of the donut shop, family members, or friends, or the customers brought in their own, a tradition started some years back by the first donut shop owners. I think you could say each cup or mug tells a story about the person who uses it." *A novel concept* I thought to myself. No real purpose, just a happening as it were, that grew and developed into a local custom.

By my own estimation the walls and overhangs contained 150-200 coffee cups and mugs. Oddly enough, each one could show a life story or a significant event in the users life. I pondered to myself, could my life be summarized on the side of a coffee cup? I had acquired and collected a few cups and mugs in my life. Hell, I thought, my personal collection could replace one fourth of these cups. I examined in retrospect my own collection of cups. No, I concluded, no one single cup in my collection could summarize my life. Each of them in order represents a single significant chapter or stage in my life. How then would all these coffee cups on the walls talk about their owners, in fragments, or complete lives? Should I imagine what the pictures or words on the cups mean or should I be so bold as to ask?

I inquired of Mary if this is something I should enjoin myself with? She suggested I could if I wanted to. It was up to me. In contemplation, I looked at my schedule through our wedding date. Two weeks this month, four weeks over the Christmas holiday and another two weeks before the wedding then we'd both be gone, living permanently in Idaho. Not enough time to become a fixture in this donut shop or have a coffee cup on the wall either. Even in my own hometown I don't frequent the local donut shop enough to partake of its local custom.

After considerable thought I decided against participating in this local custom. Adding reason to my decision was the fact we had decided to live in my home in the great northwest. A new cup here would only gather dust after the wedding and my new bride might want to join in our custom in my hometown after the wedding. Food for thought, or better yet, a toast to coffee drinkers and donut shops everywhere.

We ate breakfast in simple unhurried pleasure. I woolgathered over what I saw other customers eating. The menu was straight forward enough, the traditional hash, ham, bacon or sausage with eggs, any style, pancakes, waffles, cold or hot cereal, donuts, or croissant sandwiches. My interest was in proportions and appearance. Some of the entrees were familiar to me; however, the local names for the meals were not always so readily identifiable. I soon learned a "dropped egg" was the same as a poached egg to me. A "ranchwich" was the same as croissant. There were a few more variations but these examples give an ample idea of my interests. I settled for oatmeal and toast on this occasion and decided to become a spectator until I felt more at ease with the cuisine.

After breakfast I was introduced formally to a few of the regular customers. In particular the close circle of friends Mary normally sat at the counter with before my visit. I was pleased to meet them, each in turn and admitting up front to each person I met I hoped I could remember their names.

I was here to meet her friends and family and that meant nearly 100 new faces and voices to add to my collective memory, short as it is. Still, in time, I hoped silently I would remember their names. I wasn't sure if I could recall their names directly or use memory association.

I paid particular attention to the coffee cups each person used. I decided it would be easier if I should use memory association. The person and their coffee cup would help me to retain total recall of their individual identities. Each of their cups was very distinctive indeed.

When we left the donut shop and headed home my mind was working overtime supplanting each of these new people and their coffee cups into my memory and a history of the events of this morning. I spent most of the afternoon in this state of mind.

On Sunday we had a traditional family dinner, grandparents and parents sitting around the dining room table and the younger of the grandchildren dining at the breakfast table in the kitchen, a memory not unlike my own from my childhood (only this time I was one of the adults). I was introduced to her older daughters that had some recollection of me, their husbands and their children. Thereafter the children left for the family room in the basement, the women to tend to dinner and the men to watching football and discussing occupations. The day was warm, exhilarating and festival. I never felt I was a stranger in their midst. I felt at home.

Monday was set aside to attend the Big "E". This expression has a double meaning, Eastern States and Exposition. The six New England states of Maine, New

Hampshire, Vermont, Massachusetts, Rhode Island and Connecticut built an exposition sized fairgrounds West of Springfield, Massachusetts as a dedicated gathering site for all six states to hold and conduct an annual fair. Each state is responsible for one-sixth of the park and fairground. Each state is also charged with the maintenance and upkeep of their own buildings.

Main Street is of particular interest. Each state's headquarters building is a scaled model of that state's capital building. They make for a striking point of view as they are built on a single block and in a straight line. Patrons can walk from "State Capital" to "State Capital" in two hours time. This allows each state to exhibit its contribution to the New England area as well as the rest of the United States.

We spent our day viewing the animal exhibits, talking with carriage and wagon makers, dining on New England cuisines and watching the daily parade. (A different sponsor hosts each parade and each contained different floats and marching bands. 18 days of exposition meant 18 parades. Quite an undertaking!)

Tuesday we spent the day meeting more of her friends and her fellow workers.

On Wednesday morning we left for Vermont via scenic State Route 5 on the Vermont side of the Connecticut River.

Our destination was Island Pond near the Canadian border. Our purpose was to meet her sister-in-law and see the family summer retreat site and take in the abounding countryside. Mary concluded and correctly, I should do the sight seeing and she should do the driving.

It was on this trip Mary confided to me she couldn't read road maps very well nor did she know her left hand from her right hand. When she was married she wore her wedding ring on the left hand and her birthstone ring on her right hand. By that association she could tell left from right. She lost the association when her husband died by removing her rings. This I discovered appropriately.

At one point along State Route 5 the road parallels the Connecticut River by a stones throw (near Charlestown, New Hampshire). The bridge at this point is serviced by the only tollbooth over the river. Yes, Mary missed the turn to State Route 5. Yes, Mary drove across the bridge. And yes, the tollbooth attendant ran out of his home to collect the toll fee. Mary spent 70c to go on a round trip - around a tollbooth!

From this adventure we devised a sure fire method of determining left and right when she was driving. She wore her wedding rings on her left hand and her birthstone ring on right hand. Henceforth, we agreed wedding ring meant left turn, birthstone meant right turn. (This incident has served us well.)

Our rest stop was for pie and coffee in White River Junction at the bus station. We seated ourselves at the counter and ordered our refreshments. While seated there, an elderly gentleman dressed in well-worn schooner captain's apparel came in and sat down beside Mary. He took to talking to her like they were old friends. I assumed they were and left them alone. When the gentleman finished his coffee, talking to Mary and left, I asked her why I wasn't introduced. She said she didn't know the man at all, never got his name and had no idea who he thought he might be talking to, and at one point contemplated jumping into my lap to get away from him. I inquired, somewhat benignly, if she had had this kind of trouble meeting other men before I came along? (I knew she didn't because I couldn't get her to call me after we started corresponding. It was the man's place to call according to her upbringing.) She insisted she didn't pick up men, she didn't know how. My observation and comment to this predicament was - she didn't need to - the men came looking for her. She is a good listener. She has that "air" about her aura.

Leaving White River Junction we abandoned the idea of driving further north via State Route 5 and began using Interstate 91. I drove this part of the trip.

Our arrival in Island Pond was at sunset. We found the trailer we were to stay in for our visit. We unpacked the car; double checked the pantry supplies and then left for Island Pond's only diner, fuel for the car and a quick grocery trip. The folks in this township pull in the sidewalks early. The following morning we caught up with her sister-in-law. I was introduced to her and her husband. We visited with them for a spell and made plans for the next two days. The next evening we were invited to a home cooked meal and cards with them. The second day would consist of a drive through northern New Hampshire; a stop at a wooden covered bridge (one of very few remaining) and a Route 140 loop tour through Canada. On our last day we would resecure the trailer for the winter and depart for Springfield, Massachusetts.

Our piece of New Hampshire was a view of the Balsams Ski Resort in Dixville Notch. The resort resembles a European castle. We returned to Vermont for lunch and then we were taken to a covered wooden bridge over the Connecticut River. We strolled across the bridge and back again. From the bridge we took a short ride through a part of Canada. The landscape is replete with farms and ranches. Her relatives felt the Canadians got the better land deal in drawing up the border between the countries. I felt more on top of the world in this region than I did in Alaska when I was one mile below the Tropic of Cancer.

By Friday afternoon I was feeling very much at ease in the company of her relatives. We enjoyed a very pleasant three days in Island Pond, visiting relatives, home cooking, cards and "Sunday" drives in the middle of the week. I felt even more at home in New England. We returned to Springfield late Friday night amid a downpour of rain. The second weekend was spent performing errands, attending her church, meeting more friends and family and more importantly, visiting them in their own homes.

The second Monday we collected the keys to her boss' "other home" in Cape Cod. Mary wanted to show me more of Massachusetts, Cape Cod in particular and do some touring of the founding father's trails that later developed into the United States, as I had suggested in our talks and letters.

Our touring of Cape Cod, from Provincetown to Salem, traced the birth of the nation. Just as it was given birth and nurtured, we were born and grew together also. Our love and admiration for each other developed as a flickering flame does into a roaring bon fire. She, as the tour director, lead me through nearly 200 years of history, much of which she had taken for granted all her life. She made no remark, gave no thought, as to the significance of our walk over history's paths. Places, peoples and things she knew about as normal events became personal as we shared our thoughts and feelings over them. I awoke in her not only feelings of emotion but awareness as well. We both found something neither was looking for - another person to be a very close friend.

We viewed Nantucket Sound from the observation deck and wydows walk atop her boss' house. We dined in the company of her friends. We entertained and were entertained by them. We walked the beaches at Chatham, Provincetown and Yarmouth. And we viewed the majesty of a bustling Hyannis Port.

At Provincetown we ascended the Pilgrim Monument in a slow and steady gait, resting frequently along the way to the top (there is no elevator) and reading several memorial stones set into the mighty masonry structure. At the top we spied the expanse of the Atlantic Ocean and Cape Cod from 252 feet in the air. We also viewed the artifacts and prehistory of America in the 17th Century at its base before leaving.

After three days and nights of the mysticism which envelopes Cape Cod Province we headed north around the bay. Our second landing was the same point as the pilgrims, separatists to local historiahs, Plymouth, Massachusetts, the Plimouth Plantation and the *Mayflower II*.

Mayflower II is an actual reconstruction of the original ship. It was seven years in the making and sailed but once across the Atlantic from England to Plymouth, Massachusetts to be docked and harbored as a floating exhibit. The present ship is "manned" by 4-6 people, in era clothing, speaking era language only. The passenger area is very confining. Stooping is essential and impresses the visitors with the evidently small stature of the Pilgrims who made the original journey in 1620, 86 people confined to a small area similar to sardines in a can.

    The Plimouth Plantation is a 20th Century reconstruction of the 17th Century founding of the original Plymouth Colony. The plantation is inhabited by local citizens wearing period clothing and speaking period language. The "inhabitants" dwell in the year 1627 and know nothing of the land beyond them or the time and history of events that follow. Coal is made in fire piles. Trees are felled by axe and squared by broadax on the ground. Shingles are shaved by drawknives. Fort defenses are set above the church and pulpits. Houses are erected as they were planned and developed by the colonists 300 years before. A mock Indian village also inhabits the plantation area where canoes are made by firing out the heartwood. Modern English is allowed to be used here as the visitors could neither speak; nor understand native Indian language just as it was for the colonists themselves.

Our trip north from Plimouth to Salem took us through Boston Common and corporate Boston Township. Mary dozed off so when the highway split I took the low route - through Boston. Mary was amazed and overwhelmed by the development that had taken place in the last thirty years. She was also lost. Familiar landmarks were gone. A tunnel had replaced a bridge. It got worse but I won't elaborate.

We arrived late in the evening at Salem, our diversion through Boston consuming much time. Missing our (bypass) exit helped. We missed southern New Hampshire by five miles too.

We stayed overnight in Beverly, a township near Salem. In the morning we dined on a continental breakfast before beginning our quest of the witch hysteria in Salem.

Salem Township is much preserved in the 17th Century era. The more significant buildings remain preserved by the efforts of the local preservation societies.

Our first stop was the Witch Museum and Trials Theatre where we watched and heard tell in truth and without reservation the trials of the people accused of using witchcraft. Their accusers were all young girls from 9 to 16 years who perpetrated lies to cover up their own misdeeds. (In comparison to contemporary times this same event still occurs today. It is still hysteria but without the pomp and vigilantism of 300 years ago.) The rumor of witches being burned at the stake is a misdeed of Hollywood. None of the people who were found guilty or confessed to witchery were ever punished this way. Those that perished were locked in cells, some no bigger than a closet where, if they were fortunate, to be able to sit.

From the Witch Museum we walked to the House of the Seven Gables. It wasn't difficult to locate, we needed only to follow the red lines on the sidewalks and streets the city had painted. We toured the house with another group. It is remarkable that a structure erected in the 1700's still stands today. I stared solemnly through window glass nearly 300 years old to gaze upon the harbor as it's past owners had. It was an awesome feeling and impressed me very much.

Our continued walking would consume too much time for the rest of the day so we opted to ride the Tour Trolley to a few other places of interest. (Fittingly, the Ghostbusters Ambulance passed us on the city streets.) Among them was the church where the original trials were conducted. It is not open to the public for touring as it still functions as a church. Our time was running short so we returned to the car to continue our journey of Cape Cod Bay and the North Shore.

Mary felt inclined to show me where she spent her 15th summer. The route took us to Gloucester and the site of the Mariner Statue facing Cape Cod Bay. From there we continued on to Rockport and Cape Ann. Mary did the showing and talking and I the listening of her early childhood and experiences. I became entranced by her seemingly unmoved contacts with the history of New England. The idea enveloped me as a thick fog; How can a person living amid so much history and not be overwhelmed by it? The answer lay in simplicity. She embraced it as normal living. She had nothing to compare it with. Her sole venture away from this life-style being the three years she spent with her family in Arkansas where we first met.

Our time together touring Cape Cod Bay ended that Thursday afternoon. We were expected back in Springfield for dinner at the Colony Club at the expense of her daughters on Friday night, the eve of my departure. There, I was awestruck by a framed copy of the guest book register hanging prominently at the elevator door. The year was 1917. The names, which caught my eye, were Theodore Roosevelt Vice President of the United States and Franklin Delano Roosevelt, Undersecretary of the Department of Defense from the guest book. I felt a little out of my element of social contacts. Mary's life and culture rubbed elbows with this country's most elite historical and political characters. My life and culture was a hundred years behind hers and wallowed in the glitter and grime of Southern California.

Our dinner was a great delight. Her daughters not only paid for the meal, they also served it, a five-course meal of splendid proportions and culinary excellence.

Talk about being seduced!

My seat on the aircraft at Bradley was behind the wing and landing strut of one of those tree topping prop planes, so I couldn't see Mary standing in the window of the terminal without X-ray vision. I did turn and wave to the windows anyway even as the plane taxied to the runway. I couldn't distinguish any people let alone features. I felt a sourness building in the pit of my stomach.

I gave myself stomach cramps at the prospect of leaving. I had been happy again. The prospect of going home, alone, and resuming a life of solitude was disheartening. Added to this feeling of emptiness was the future of our happiness and the final report card of my acceptance into her world by her family and friends.

Chapter 12

Promises To Keep

"A promise to one's self is the most important."

Reflecting on the Past

Following my trip to New England I predisposed myself to making more changes in my life and life-style and keeping the promises I had made. The hominess of Mary's life-style appealed to me very much. Her family and friends were warm and sincere. The countryside and its history abounded. I found my attitude improved. A lot of the shadows and mists concealing her life from my vision were dissipated.

My trip to Massachusetts and the visit with Mary helped me to focus on the promises I had made to Betty, to myself and to my family. I felt less guilty about the prospects of marrying again. In the beginning of my affair with Angela I felt some infidelity from Betty, in our case the infidelity was focused more on Mary's late husband. I was apprehensive I could overcome the concept of loving another man's wife because I once knew him personally.

The trip brought me to the conclusion I could marry again and this time with Betty's blessing if she were present to tell me. A life alone was not my destiny. Marriage was. Overcoming my feelings of infidelity to Mary's late husband would require more time.

For me to get on with living the time had come to separate myself more from my past. The excess baggage of a past into a new future was not welcome. The promises made to Betty, myself and my family should be carried out.

Promises to Betty

The vow of, "till death do us part" finally had for me, meant till death do us part and no more. My love and adoration for Betty had not and will not wane; it must however draw to a close. Whatever love we shared for one another is gone. It cannot be shared after death. It took two to make it exist. One cannot carry it on to eternity.

As it was our pact and Betty's desire for me to go on with living and not alone, I found the guilty feelings that I built up in depression vanquishing in light of my feelings for Mary. These feelings were newer and quite different from the feelings I held for Betty. Those feelings Betty knew me better than anyone and knew what would be best for me seem to have waned at last. A whole new field of emotions engulfed me.

Promises to Myself

I recalled my past encounters with girls and women of my younger days. Each one of them aroused different feelings and emotions in me for different reasons. I also recounted the words of wisdom I wrote to Mary in one of my letters when playing devil's advocate for her daughters blessings on a possible life together.

We don't just love one person or one way. In our lifetime, we meet and fall in love with several people of the opposite sex. We courted the concept of a happy life ever after with all of our encounters, dates and engagements. In the end, we choose to marry but one person. That person being the one who allows us most to remain ourselves and chooses to grow with us.

I had fallen or been in love with a dozen or so girls and women in my life, but for one reason or another those relationships could not progress to a deeper level required for marriage, thus they ended.

In our relationship, Mary's and mine, the barriers we encountered were more like speed bumps than walls. We did have our differences; philosophical and emotional, however, they are minor compared to our previous marriages. This condition exists because we are starting our life together from a far more distant point in our ages. We both bring greater education and experience into an impending marriage whereas in our former marriages we both began from youth and untried skills. We likewise have less time to compensate for errors, thus we are less apt to make them.

Promises to My Family

In meeting Mary I also kept a renewed promise for my family. I met a woman who does place family first. This above all makes her the most desirable woman I ever met. She loves and cares about children and grandchildren very much. I didn't ask for anything more.

THE PROMISE

"Across the years I will walk with you -

In deep, green forests; on shores of sand;

And when our time on earth is through,

in heaven, too, you will have my hand."

- Robert Sexton
Journeys of the Human Heart

Chapter 13

Keeping My Vows

"Change is the only constant."

More Changes

My life and love with Betty I drew to a close. From the moment of her death to my realization another lifestyle was before me, via bereavement, my life and love for the rest of my days settled on changing, my habits and customs and compromises to yet another lifestyle and another woman.

I Found Another Woman When I Wasn't Looking

I had to put my past life and love behind me. I had to learn to live again and not just survive. There was a newer and brighter hope of another level of happiness to be enjoyed and experienced ahead of me. Far from what I had known with any of the other women I dated or courted; Farther yet from what I had known with Betty and Angela.

Comparisons between women are deadly. They are deadly for a multitude of reasons. Each woman considers herself special; each woman is her own identity; each woman has her own personality; and each woman is educated and taught a set of values and principles by which she grows and matures. I erred in the beginning of my quest for another woman to share my life with by failing to recognize these facts. My major mistake was in comparing one to another. Trying to pick the best from each and making them over into what I wanted or needed. In looking, I found disappointment brought out by expectation. When I stopped looking so intently, I met who I was looking for.

In a divorce the decision to live alone would have been mine to make. With death, the decision was thrust upon me whether I was ready for it or not. I hate to say I survived, better to say I adjusted to my new role. I made the correct decisions for the correct reasons. I was not without errors in arriving at those decisions, but neither did I perpetuate the errors I made into a worse mess. I learned from them. My courtship of Angela was a sincere if misguided and faulty attempt at easing my pain - and hers too for that matter. We both misjudged loneliness and sympathy for love and admiration. We wanted to live alone - together. That was no basis for a stable and ongoing relationship. The time to reexamine my vow to marry or remain single was upon me.

Courtship and marriage can and should be romantic and caring, however, romance is not the corner stone by which a marriage thrives. It thrives on loyalty, trustworthiness and fidelity, being a helpmate, sacrifice, conversation, family, compatibility, principles and values. Real love comprises all of these elements. My vow to find another friend to fulfill life's journey had to encompass these qualities above romance.

The physical attraction is a separate need from these qualities. Physical love is a learned quality between two people. Neither is born with the knowledge of how to make love. Each partner teaches the other - each partner learns from the other. Love and marriage conceived in a physical attraction is doomed to failure because once the physical attraction is ended so is the marriage. My vow to set aside my feelings of fidelity to a deceased woman proved the most difficult.

This was an overriding concern and philosophy I entered into my first marriage with. It sustained our marriage through a period of time when divorce cases reached an all time high in this country. In retrospect, when I attended school as a child, classmates with single parents were a minority. Virtually every single parent classmate acquired that title by death. In the twenty years that followed, from high school graduation, through military service, to retirement, this social condition reversed itself. I had the auspicious occasion to send my daughters to all of the schools I attended as a child for a brief period at the conclusion of my military career. They had the distinction of being the only children in school, with both Parents still married AND still living together, they were treated by other classmates as goddesses. They were reveled by other classmates as the luckiest kids in school.

Setting Better Standards

My vows to keep were restored by reading a book on romance. It was written by a woman, for women, but I felt if I was to succeed at finding another woman to share the rest of my life's journey with, I must know how a woman thinks and acts. This particular book contained some chapters on issues I gave little thought about. It was from these concepts I refocused my attention towards women in general and to tailor a guide by which I could recognize and identify a woman more capable and able to fulfill my needs as well as her own.

My affair with Angela taught me the family of my own creation was important to me, far more than a second or successive wife. I had given in temporarily to her sultry concepts children should have no effect or bearing on second mates. That is not true. They have a very profound affect. A second mate can divide or multiply a successive marriage. I had learned the hard way, by experience, family is more important than another wife or a significant other. Hence I created a one-item list of positive qualities a second wife should abide by and I as well - First Families First. If this aspect of a relationship worked, the entire prospect would be worth pursuing.

On the negative side, the list was narrowed to four items only. No smoking, no drinking, no gambling and no children.

The no smoking rule was for the betterment of my health as well as her own. The featured articles about second hand smoke and my health made it automatic.

The no drinking rule was raised to a higher level because of my affair with Angela. Drinking had made the decided reason for terminating our relationship. The cause and effects were too stressful. The cost was too prohibitive.

The no gambling rule was a safeguard against squandering. I had made my lifestyle comfortable by not wasting money away on speculation. When compared to the harder forms of gambling, cards, dice, keno and one-armed bandits, even a state lottery is a losing proposition.

The no children rule meant several things; first of all - no second families. While I toyed with the idea initially, I couldn't bring myself to the prospect of raising another family in my senior years. My health wouldn't allow it. Summarily, I didn't want a second marriage that included thirty to forty-year-old children still living at home with a surviving parent. Even younger children from ten to twenty would prove too demanding on my health.

So there it was, the lists of negotiable and nonnegotiable items to form the basis of a new relationship and or marriage. These ideas, coupled with the vows and pacts I made with Betty and myself formed the ideology by which I investigated and courted other women.

And so I did. I made mistakes, over and over, but this list kept me on track. I saw, dated and courted many other women during my bereavement. They were wonderful as friends and companions but no real reason for a life of matrimony. There wasn't anything any of them did to disqualify themselves so much as what I learned from them about myself and the potential consequences of a long-term relationship between us.

Don't Live Alone - Get Married Again

I had weighed heavily the decision to meet with and court more women following my experience with Angela. The affair steered me away from divorcees. Instead I chose to examine the aura and potential of dating and courting widows for a time, then to consider, coldly and logically, the positives and negatives of both. From this plan I would make a decision whether to remain single or to actively engage in a companionship worthy of marriage. Setting better standards was the path to follow.

I "courted" two widows simultaneously for a while following my break up with Angela. It was a dangerous thing to do but I tried it. I kept both women separated from each other physically and mentally while examining the personalities and principles and values of both. They were remarkably alike but one aspect was different. One had courage, the other didn't. It was from this singular point I made my decision to marry one of them.

Oddly enough, my most innocent and sincerest of female contacts turned out to be a woman geographically removed from me. Locations aside, everything else worked splendidly. Mary and I developed a rapport by mail I thought only being and living together would provide. I overlooked the fact distance could be a positive factor.

As it turned out distance was the most positive factor of our relationship. We had been separated by time and geography for over thirty years. Our letters had brought us together spiritually, the long distance phone calls emotionally and finally airline tickets physically. Our relationship was founded in a casual meeting in time, years ago, held together by pen-pal letters between wives and brought back together through mutual grief circumstances. Time and distance, what subtle partners!

My letters and visits with Mary brought me to the conclusion I would not continue to live alone. I should and would marry again - to her. Our relationship was stable. And by the list I had developed she scored the highest.

I proposed to Mary a second time and she accepted. Our value time together had been limited but it made little difference to our mutual decision. We were "psychically connected" from the beginning of our letters and later in our exchanged visits.

Chapter 14

A New Direction

"A path taken is a path left behind."

The Cause and Effects of Change

Between Mary's visit with me on New Years 1995 to my visit with her on Christmas 1995 I observed and discovered more of the differences and similarities between her and me. Through them I made some comparisons too. Betty and I were totally equal and opposite in virtually every respect. Still we came together as two pieces of a jigsaw puzzle. What we lacked however was the picture. We encompassed the physical and structural shapes to bond together but the colors of the pieces rarely matched, it didn't begin that way, it developed over time.

Change is Better For Succeeding Marriages

Betty's medical condition prohibited many of the events we enjoyed early in our married life. The condition in her leg inhibited her ability to work, travel, hike, walk, dance, or merely prolonged standing. She became in part, a couch potato. She spent long hours engaged in reading, painting, crocheting, cross stitching, needle pointing, quilting and similar lap types of work and hobbies. This left me with little to do but to find similar work and hobbies so the two of us could spend quality time together. I took to reading, modeling and painting. Our culinary desires were as opposite as our personalities. Our values and principles were so entwined I left those decisions nearly totally up to her.

By comparison, Mary was still active, healthy and uninhibited by those restraints. She was able to work, enjoyed the outdoors, walking, hiking and dancing. She was a venturer, traveler and tourist. Sitting at home was boring. We found by dining together we had similar culinary tastes. Our principles were similar and although our approaches to complex problems more diverse, they still provided the desired outcome.

Through these differences and similarities I learned to love again albeit from an opposing point of view. I found in Mary a slightly older, more mature and more experienced woman to my liking. We endeared the same philosophy and value and held it in the highest esteem, family.

Geography separated us, her to the east and me to the west, a cultural shock that could undermine most relationships. With us it proved itself an asset. She had spent nearly all of her life in New England while I had spent nearly all of my life in the "Far West." Our desire to visit each other's domain was and remains strong. This condition gave us both what we wanted, travel and tourism and a home on each coast.

After Betty's passing I wanted to get back into living as a couple as soon as possible so all might return to being normal again and before I had reason to believe loneliness was all that was left to living out my own life. Time and other relationships with other women proved to me how wrong I was. The healing process takes much longer. I went out grasping at skirts, looking for a woman who closest suited my dreams and would pick up where my previous relationship had ended. It doesn't work that way.

21 Again At Age 53

As I began my emotional trip back to my adolescence I discovered a path taken is a path left behind. To begin a new journey a new starting point or an established starting point was necessary. The established point, Betty's date of death was wrong so I went back to the emotional age of 21 with the experienced age of 50 to begin my quest. It was while I was in this stasis I met Mary who was also widowed. I rediscovered through her, a man does not love but once or only one way. He loves each woman differently and for different reasons. I found in her so many more characteristics to my liking and another level of happiness.

I had "proposed" to Mary in more than one way, informally and formally. Informally I made succinct remarks and comments, which I felt, were innocent in passing conversation, only to find out later some women took them as proposals and intent, those being, cleaning this house and living in Idaho with me. Mary certainly did. Formally I had asked her to marry me outright, even immediately, to the point of elopement. Fortunately, she elected to wait and think it over logically, an attribute, a blessing and a highly desirable trait. Time was in our favor for emotional ties and bonds.

From a Pen-Pal to a Companion

We made plans to be married March 9, 1996 in Springfield, Massachusetts and to reside in Idaho. Through a series of discussions and compromises and concessions (mostly mine), we arrived at this date and location. The location was the merit of the bride. She had lived and worked in this area for nearly thirty years. The wedding is for all obvious reasons, the bride's day of honor. She had a longer and larger entourage to commemorate our marriage. I, on the other hand, had but a handful. The wedding would take place in her church with a reception to follow; it would be photographed by her friends for posterity. Both circumstances satisfied my latent desires and the voids of my first marriage. Idioms aside, the date held a curious fact also. Most of the circumstances surrounding our meetings, letters, trips and families focused on, or were divisible by three (or almost)- the tabloid looks like this:

First marriage duration (hers)	33
First marriage duration (mine)	29
Our ages in the year of our marriage	60 & 54
Age difference	6
Month and year born	3-36
	6-42
Number of children (both of us-all girls)	6

Number of grandchildren (hers)	6
Number of grandchildren (mine)	3
Number of letters written (by each of us)	69
Number of greeting cards (each)	36
Number of visits (to each other)	3
Number of the month meeting each other's families (Dec - Sep)	12 & 9
Numbers comprising wedding date (incidentally a leap year making the date the 69th day of the year)	3-9-96
Number of attendees at our wedding	96
Date departed Springfield	3-13-96
Number of days in the honeymoon	9
Number of miles driven	3300
Date arrived in Mountain Home	3-21-96

The beat goes on but by this list the point is made.

Chapter 15

Living Happily Ever After - Again

"Because - it feels so right."

M.L.

Our Reasons For Marriage

Because of our letters, our visits, our past, our likes, our dislikes, our desires, our wants and most importantly our needs, Mary and I consented to marriage. We found in each other the companionship we both wanted. We found in each other a new soul mate. I consider myself very lucky to have met Mary when I did. She brought me back to being myself again, the person I was before I met and married Betty, not the person I was at the time of Betty's death.

Being Psychically Connected

Because of my trips to Massachusetts I convinced myself Mary was the right woman for me and for the rest of life. I found in her all the attributes I needed in resuming the matrimonial state. She, in her own way, felt as I did. Through our letters and cards and visits we had developed a rapport as a couple. We also learned that we communicated in another way; I called it cosmically connected, a nondescript term in contemporary English but adequate to our purposes and understanding. Essentially it meant for us, we felt and knew what each other was thinking about saying or doing when being together or miles apart. It's an element of understanding normally attributed to couples having lived together for 25 years or more, an intertwining of idiosyncrasies of each other's personalities and habits.

Embracing Companionship

Because our love for each other grew out the basic needs and compliments each provided the other a companionship developed. I say compliments, not in the social graces sense, but in the fitting of two jigsaw puzzle pieces together. Physical attributes aside, we also made a picture. Her weaknesses were my strong points and vice versa. We also observed some of the undesirable and annoying habits of our former mates were gone and forgotten and entertained some of the more desirable traits needed for our companionship were present.

Our Wedding Transcript

Because our being together felt so right we were married. Here is the wedding transcript, as it happened and as recorded by the church.

    A musical prelude is played as guests arrive and are seated.

    The Processional goes forth led by the youngest grandchildren, our children and trailed by the bride and the groom.

    A Wedding Bell Carillon sounds as all are seated and the pastor enters. His sermon begins:

"Dear friends, we have joined together today in the presents of God and with you, to join this man and this woman in holy marriage which is instituted by God, regulated by his commandments, blessed by our Lord Jesus Christ and, to be held in honor among all people. Let us therefore remember, that God has established and sanctified marriage to provide for the welfare and the happiness of the human family. For this reason our Savior has declared that a man shall leave his father and his mother and cleave to his wife and the two shall become as one. By His apostles He has instructed those who enter into this relation to cherish a mutual esteem and love, to share in each other's infirmities and weaknesses, to comfort each other in sickness and trouble and sorrow, to provide for each other in their household, to pray for and encourage each other and to live together as heirs of the grace of life. As we are (gathered) together today to witness the joining of Eugene Campbell and Mary Laitres, we do so in a contact of a worship service together. That we will be worshipping God and thanking Him for his many goodness's. To us particularly, the goodness of love and marriage and their happiness, we pray these two (people) will enjoy all the rest of their days. So, with that in mind, I'd like to ask for you to join me in prayer as we ask God's presence upon this gathering today.

"Our gracious Heavenly Father it is only by your presence we might know the joy of any occasion and it is only by your favor that we might have joy in any relationship. We pray today you will be especially gracious and be present and favorable to us as we join together. May our singing, may our attendance to the word and may our sharing in the joy Eugene and Mary have already begun, be complete today because you have been with us and continue to go with us. It is in Christ's name that we pray. Amen."

"Would you please turn in your red hymnal that is in the rack before you to (hymn) number 28. That is the song that Mary and Gene have chosen for this occasion, "To God Be the Glory, Great Things He Has Done."

After singing the hymnal, the pastor asks the congregation to be seated.

"A wedding and a marriage become a Christian wedding, a Christian marriage, not just because they are (performed) in a Christian church, not just because a Christian minister performs the ceremony, not even because the persons involved are Christians themselves. It is because the couple determines that they will perform their duties for one another, built and based, upon the word of God. And so, as Gene and Mary come together today, it is our desire to set some standards as (is) our foundation (and) to set their relationship (which is) based upon love.

"I want to read three passages for our consideration today. The first comes from the book of Genesis, Chapter four, verse 25. The Lord God said it is not good for the man to be alone. I will provide a partner for him. So God formed out of the ground all the wild animals and the birds of heaven and brought them to the man to see what he would call them.

And whatever the man called them, that was their name. The man gave names to all the cattle, (and) birds of heaven, but for the man himself no partner had been found. So the Lord God put the man into a deep trance. And while he slept, he took one of the ribs and closed the flesh over its place. The Lord then built up the rib, which he had taken out of the man into a woman. He brought her to the man. And the man said, now at last, bone from my bones, flesh from my flesh, this shall be called woman. For it was from man she was taken. This is why a man leaves his father and mother and is united to his wife and the two become one flesh. And the man and his wife were both naked and were not ashamed. Because (when) we say as we are getting married we will love one another and we're building our marriage upon a relationship of love, it is good for us from time to time to hear how God's word describes this emotion love.

"Saint Paul writes to us in First Corinthians, verse 13 in familiar passage, but it does well for me to remember and I think for you as well; Love is patient and kind; Love is not jealous or boastful, is not arrogant or rude. Love does not insist upon on its own way. It is not irritable or resentful. It does not rejoice at wrong but rejoices at the right. Love bears all things, believes all things, hopes all things, endures all things. Love never ends. As for prophecy it will pass away. As for tongues they will cease. As for knowledge it will pass away, for knowledge is imperfect. Our prophecy is imperfect. And when perfect comes, the imperfect will pass away. When I was a child I spoke as a child. As a child I thought as a child, I reasoned as a child. When I became a man I gave up childish things. For now we see in a mirror, dimly, but then face-to-face I know in part, then I shall understand fully, even as I have been fully understood. So, faith, love and hope abide these three. But the greatest of these is love.

"And then again from the book of Ephesians. From the pen of Saint Paul under the inspiration and inspection God's Holy Spirit we read these words; be subject to one another out of the reverence of Christ. Wives be subjects to your husbands, as to the Lord, for the husband (is) the head of the wife, as Christ is the head of the church. His body and is Himself its Savior. As the church is subject to Christ, so let wives also be subject in everything to their husbands. Husbands love your wives as Christ loved the church and gave Himself up for her that he might sanctify her. Having cleansed her by the washing of water, the word, the church might be presented before Him in splendor without spot or wrinkle or any such thing, that she might be holy and without blemish. Even so, husbands should love their wives as their own bodies. He who loves his wife loves himself. For no man ever hates his own flesh but nourishes it and cherishes it as Christ does for the church. And, because we are members of His body, for this reason shall a man leave his father and his mother and be joined to his wife and the two shall become as one. It's a great mystery and I take it to mean Christ and the church. However, let each of you love his wife as himself and let the wife see that she respects her husband.

"I'm always struck when I come to the passage in Genesis of the creation. I'm always struck with the fact that through each day of creation after God had thrown the stars and the moon and the sun in its place, after He had divided the land from the water, after he caused the shrubbery and vegetation to come forth, after He had created (the) fish and animals (how) on each day of creation He said, 'It is good. It is good. It is good.' And when God said something is good, it is really great! And yet when He created the man He didn't say it was good. He said it is not good. Now none of us need take a moment, none of us need to think for a moment, that God is saying the creation of man himself was not good. What he said, 'It is not good for the man to be alone.' So God did something about it. God took the loneliness, the emptiness, the incompleteness of Adam's heart and experience and filled that for him.

"Another thing he did first however He took Adam aside and he allowed all of the animals of creation to pass before him. All. I think what God was doing here was saying, Adam, see if you can find someone who will fill your loneliness, someone who will be what you need. Some of us are of the generation who would remember a rock and roll group whose name was Three Dog Night. That might be something that is (more) familiar to us. Maybe though, some of us don't know where the name Three Dog Night came from. In Australia, some of the aboriginal tribes count the coldness of the night by how many dogs it takes to keep them warm. A one-dog night is sort of cool night, a two-dog night a lot colder, last night I think would be a four or five dog night. But God brought all the animals in front of Adam and said, 'See if you can find someone here to fulfill that loneliness, that incompleteness in your heart.' Any one of us could identify with Adam that feeling of being alone, without a mate and any one of us could agree with God that it is not good that I should be alone.

"I've played with this in my mind from time to time, to think how it might have gone, Adam, looking at all the animals as they came by him thinking, oh, this could be good one. Here comes the king of beasts, the lion and Adam thinking, well, the king of beasts is powerful, a good hunter, can bring me food, protect me from predators, or any enemy, but, then he's thinking more, the king of beasts has a very loud roar a I don't think I want that in my home, a lot of roaring.

"Maybe then the ox came by. Here's this large, strong animal. Some of us have been to Sturbridge Village and seen them, been astounded by their size and their shoulders are about this high. The strongest animal you can imagine and Adam certainly had that thought. An ox is someone I could have as a partner. But, although the ox is strong and of great endurance, the ox doesn't talk. It doesn't have any communication skills.

"So it is not good for man to be alone. We could go on. Uh, one other animal I think about is the elephant. It's big, lumbering and strong. Powerful as the elephant is we often think of it in terms of memory. I only bring up the elephant Gene because there are certain things we need to remember. One of those is March 10th, another is Mother's Day and another is Mary's birthday. I'm sorry-I meant to say (today) March 9th. Want to check the date on that marriage license to see if I put the right date on there? There are some things you'll want to forget, hurt feelings, strife and failure.

"All of this is to say when all the animals passed before Adam none of them was found to be a suitable helper or mate for him. So God caused a great sleep to come upon Adam and some people think men have been asleep during all the important events in their lives ever since. That's not exactly true. Man was put into a deep trance and God took a rib from his side and built up a woman. The word that is used for built up is the same kind of word used for someone who is custom building a home, or custom building a unique one of a kind model of anything. As you two come together today, my reminder to you is, remember each of you is custom built for one another. Custom made.

"Gene you look at Mary, dressed up, stunningly beautiful. Think of her today as a gift wrapped present from God, designed and built just for you. And Mary, the same thing, think of Gene as a stunningly handsome, gift wrapped present from God for you. You (both) need to think about this often. There might be times when you'll think you didn't get such a prize. But, you'll come back the next day, thankful that God gave you one another. This allows you to have patience with one another. To accept each other as you are.

"One of my favorite Latin's comes from the first Rocky Movies. In that movie you remember the guy Rocky can hardly talk. He falls in love with a young girl who never talks. And one of his buddies says, "What do you see in her?" Big ole Rocky replies, "We got gaps." His buddy says, "What do you mean we got gaps?" Rocky brings his hands together saying, "We got gaps." That's how you two are coming together.

"It's not good for somebody to be alone. You've already proven that. You were (both) alone, you were married and you became alone again. You (both) know better than I can describe, the aloneness and the separateness, but God has brought us together to fulfill those gaps in each other's lives. So build on those. Appreciate those (gaps).

"It's not good for a man to be alone. You are custom built for one another and notice this too, that the bible says, a man and a woman should leave their parents, to cleave or stick like glue to one another. Now that hardly applies to either of you, leaving your parents. You've already proven you can do that.

"But there are over a dozen people sitting behind you who really are trying to be happy today, because their parents are leaving them. You're getting married to one another. For those that are here, as family members I know this is a difficult, bittersweet day, to see mom leave, for you three Laitres daughters to see mom pack up and go to a place called Idaho. Does anyone know where Idaho is? Uh, that's where your mom will be. For the grandkids, you've had grandma with you all your lives. All of a sudden she's going away. Could you (all) remember one thing? That your mom, dad, grandma, grandpa, are going to be very happy together. The greatest gift you can give to them is to say mom, dad, I love you so much, I want you to go and love each other. We're going to pray for you and encourage you and give you an invitation to come back anytime you want.

"A man and a woman leave to cleave but it's very difficult when it's the children letting go of their parents. I can't imagine what it's like to say goodbye to my children. I've two daughters who, on some of my better days, hope they never get married. On other days, I can't wait that they will. But, to say good-bye, it's going to be tough for all of you. May you understand your parents joy at this time as well. U-m-m, Gene, you and Mary give us gift by showing us, how God operates in the human family. All around us marriages are disintegrating, people mistreat and betray one another, but, by being Christians in marriage you have the opportunity to show us what Saint Paul said, 'A man would love his wife in order that the world might see how Christ loves us.' My prayer for you as pastor is that as folks look at you all the days of your lives that they'll see love, commitment and faithfulness, so if anyone ever asks you why is that, you can tell them God has loved us, has been committed to us and faithful to us and we want to give that gift back to each other, our kids, grandkids and to all the world.

"I want to thank you all for coming today and witnessing this ceremony for Gene and Mary. I'm personally, absolutely delighted. You could have knocked me over with a feather Mary, 6 months ago, when she caught me in the hall in back of the church and told me what was going to happen. She was going to get married (again)- When I say I was knocked over, I mean I didn't have a clue. But, I was absolutely happy. When I say you two have been given to one another as a gift from God I was just delighted to see how He's worked things out together, so you'll both have happiness and joyfulness in your lives once again.

"In lieu of saying the Lord's Prayer together, we're going to listen to it sung. The part of the prayer I think most significant is; Thy will be done, on Earth, as it is in Heaven. May the will of God always be done in your marriage. May you always know his blessing and happiness each day of your lives together.

The Soloist sings the Lord's Prayer.

We exchanged our vows. We lit the Unity Candle. The soloist sings again, this time, "There is Love." Pastor Burk declares we are married. He offers a closing prayer then presents us as newly weds to our guests and witnesses and families. We walked back down the center aisle as man and wife graciously accepting the congratulations of the congregation. A musical postlude hails our departure from the sanctuary. We are followed to the reception hall for dinner, blessings, pictures, gifts and cutting the wedding cake.

CAMPBELL FAMILY NEWSLETTER

SPECIAL EDITION - MARCH 1996

Greetings family and friends everywhere,

Well, guess what? After 3300 miles, 9 days, 27 meals, 6 boxes of Girl Scout Cookies, $900.00 and 0 arguments while confined in a car and sleeping in a different bed every night we arrived safely in Mountain Home 21 Mar 96. Is everything still divisible by 3?

We left Springfield shortly after noon on 13 Mar 96. We drove west on Interstate 90 passing through the Berkshires amid numerous frozen waterfalls of runoff melting snows along the Mass Pike.

Our trip through New York State was a sorrowful site as we passed by numerous old run down and abandoned farms littering the countryside like so much wind blown debris. It's a pity. We arrived in Buffalo shortly after dusk. Our driving plan was to alternate every four hours so Mary could take a nap. I would drive early in the morning, Mary in the afternoon and me again in the evening if we would still be on the road by dark. So much for the best of intentions. Mary was still driving come sunset on day one. She's a good driver with a questionable navigator. After we crossed the

Rainbow Bridge we went directly to the Falls. We were blessed with the start of the night light spectacle and a parking ticket. Canadian police don't wait long. The weather in Canada was cold and wintery and windy. Good cuddling conditions. The Falls were laden with snow and ice but the water was still flowing. The *Maid of the Mist* was dry docked by the ice pack around the boathouse. We spent the night in the Holiday Inn on the Canadian side. In the morning I commented to Mary that the water (The Falls) was left on all night. Despite the distance of the hotel from the Falls they were clearly audible all night. In the morning we returned for a daylight look and a daylight photo shoot of the Falls. Before leaving Niagara Falls for Michigan I gassed up the car. The navigator ninny told the attendant to fill up the tank. THAT tank of gas cost more than the hotel room, dinner, or breakfast. Stop laughing.

 While still in shock from the gas station we headed for Michigan. We drove beside Lake Superior until Hamilton, and then turned westward for Port Huron. The infamous Orange Barrel Highway exists even in Canada. The speed limit in Canada is 60 MPH, if you're dumb enough to travel that slowly. Across parts of the province we tried to keep up with the trucks. Ho, ho, ho, our needle was pegged at 85 MPH and we were still passed by everything, cars, trucks and telephone poles. We crossed back into the good old USA at

Port Huron, Michigan and stopped for lunch. Lancaster, Michigan was similar to New York State in many regards. We rented a room in Flint and drove to Frankenmuth. Mary wanted to visit Bronners Christmas Wonderland and have the (all you can eat) chicken dinner at Zehnder's Bavarian Haus. It's old country atmosphere and decor and the servants wear period costumes. The dinner was a great delight. We also listened to the 35 bell carillon in the Bavarian Inn's Glockenspiel Tower and watched the carved wooden figures depicting the Pied Piper outside the Bavarian Inn. Nearby is a replica of a 19th Century Holz Brucke (wooden covered bridge) that spans the Cass River. Again the weather was windy, chilly and good for cuddling.

We left Flint, Michigan in the morning to traverse a brief section of northwestern Indiana. As it was afternoon Mary drove this leg of the journey. In Indiana, short of the Illinois state line traffic was bumper to bumper before it came to a halt. I don't believe Mary has ever had the experience of stopping on one of nations longest parking lots before. She did a lot of talking to herself and anyone else that would listen. Stuff happens in the big auto happy cities. The stop and go traffic finally got to the source of the problem, a truck in the emergency lane. His brakes had locked up, caught fire and cremated the tractor and trailer. The diversion was sufficient for Mary to miss the exit to

Rochelle and we took a 1 1/2 hour side trip of suburbia Chicago!!! Chicago traffic on Friday at 4:00 PM! Mary was not a happy camper. New York City was looking pretty good. We also saw more of Lake Michigan than was planned. Driving returned to "normal" back on the toll road. We got back an hour of our delay crossing into the Central time zone. We arrived in Rochelle shortly before dark.

In Rochelle we visited with Mary's cousin. We were received with hugs and kisses and dinner and conversation, most of which revolved around the family tree. Mary updated the family bible for them. We spent the night and had a country breakfast in the morning and then went to see the old family estate in Malta. A few additions to the old house but basically unchanged over the years.

We left Illinois temporarily to go to Centerville, Iowa. My father's side of the family originated from there. I took a few photos of gravestones and made some notes for my family genealogy. Then we drove back to Illinois, this time to Quincy where my parents were raised, married and lived for a few years and my grandparents are buried. I took photographs of the headstones and made some genealogy notes then we left for Hannibal, Missouri.

In Hannibal we took the tour of the Mark Twain Cave south of town. We walked through 3/4 of a mile of tunnels that comprise the cave. I'd seen it twice before 33 years ago as a young man. Mary had never seen it nor knew it really existed. Samuel Clemens, aka Mark Twain, included the cave in his book, the Adventures of Tom Sawyer. We saw the original entrance, the Lemon Squeeze passage, the Parlor, the Post Office, the James Gang hideout, Injun Joe's treasure trove, the Pantry, the Wedding Corner, the Stone Falls and all the other sites mentioned in Twain's book. After the cave tour we went to old town Hannibal, glimpsed at the wax museum, met a lady whose son lives in Boise and promised to drop in and say hello for her, Becky Thatcher's House, Samuel Clemens fathers office, the infamous white picket fence and a few of the other sites Clemens used in his stories along the Mississippi River. The riverboat was downstream in New Orleans for the winter. From Hannibal we drove to Independence, Missouri, the home of Harry Truman. The legal speed limit on Interstate 70 is 70 MPH. Catch me if you can and everyone did! We felt like we were back in Canada, too slow to be in the fast lane. We opted not to drive into Independence until morning. We arrived in time for breakfast. We toured the outside of the Truman Home. It is closed on Monday's for cleaning and maintenance. We toured the Truman Library and the Queen City Interpretive Center of the Oregon Trail beginning in Independence.

  We decided to make a course change in Kansas City and to drive through Kansas to Denver as opposed to heading north to Nebraska. Our visits and touring in Illinois, Iowa and Missouri used up a lot of time and part of my family was waiting for us in Colorado. In Kansas we drove through rolling plains, farmland and oil pumpers. We spent the night in Oak Grove and woke up to snow on the car. This was the only bad weather we encountered on the trip. We stopped in Colby 17 miles further west to shop at the Factory Outlet stores and for breakfast. We both bought coats and shoes. By 10:00 am the road was clear and suitable for travel. I pointed out to Mary the gates across the highway and the on-ramps. Yes, Kansas and Colorado do close their highways during severe weather and they make sure no dummies try to get through when the road is unsafe.

We stopped in Limon, Colorado for lunch and met a woman who lived in Mountain Home a few years back. They left there to be closer to her family. We arrived in Denver about 4:00 pm. I took Mary on a tour of Fitzsimmons Army Hospital Base east of town. We went commissary shopping for road treats and then to the Post Exchange for birthday gifts. We spent the night with a cousin of the family and in the morning went on a brief tour of what is left of old Lowry Air Force Base and to visit my sister in laws on the west side of town. We departed Denver about noon heading north up Interstate 25. Eight miles this side of the Wyoming border we saw three herds of buffalo grazing in the plains.

Westward on Interstate 80 we spotted three small herds of grazing antelope. Crossing Wyoming was easy; the speed limit is 75 MPH!

In Utah we picked up Interstate 84 west, connecting the dots from Interstate 84 east. You might say at this point the distance between them could be called Mary's Bog. An inside joke. As we crossed northeastern Utah we were back above the snowline. We saw more snow along this section of the trip than anywhere else. The temperature in Utah was 70 degrees - with snow still in the mountains. I let Mary do the driving across the Idaho state line. In Twin Falls we stopped at the suspension bridge over the Snake River. I showed Mary the city's Municipal Golf Course down below on the Snake River. We walked under the bridge to the other side and viewed the Snake River from both perspectives. We crossed the Snake River using the bridge unlike Evil Knivel who wanted to jump it at a point above the golf course 20 years ago. From the bridge we drove towards Mineral Hot Springs for a leisurely dip in the "hot tub." We used the Caprice to help herd a runaway steer back to his farm en route to the springs. Welcome to the great northwest Mary! Yes, Mary recovered enough to take at least one picture.

We arrived home Thursday night about 9:30 pm. It took two hours to unload the car, scan the answering machine, plow through the moving cartons and glance through the mail.

Friday morning we went to Mountain Home AFB. I went to the Job Fair being sponsored by the base and we both picked up some job applications for consideration. I took Mary to the club for the traditional Friday luncheon, smorgasbord. Friday afternoon my grandkids came over to see "Papa" and Mary. Friday night I took Mary to bingo, Idaho style. She won one game playing for me for $50.00 and her name was drawn for one of the two birthday prizes, another $50.00. Beginner's luck! Saturday we spent most of the day unpacking moving cartons. In the evening we went to dinner on Mary's birthday prize. I cornered a waitress and Mary got a birthday dessert and a quartet of waiters and waitresses singing to her "Happy Birthday."

Today is Sunday. Mary spent most of the day unpacking and I spent most of the day sorting mail and paying all the bills from the last four weeks. We're down to the last four moving cartons.

That's the trip folks. Drop us line when the mood strikes and we'll do our best to do the same. Thanks for everything. We had a great trip. Love to all.

         Uge - Mar

Postscript I

If everything in my life has been centered on the "middle" theme then I hope to believe this is the middle of my life. My first fifty years has been spent with one woman and one lifestyle. As such I hope the sequel to this story won't be printed for another fifty years and that your great-grand children will know how this marriage comes out.

Epilogue

I met and dated six women following the death of Betty who made an influence on my decision to remain single or remarry. This then is how they fared after sharing a part of their lives with me and I a part of my life with them.

Dora continued her education and graduated. She retired from the military and married (again) and moved to another state. It is my fervent wish this relationship becomes the one she has searched for and it becomes her.

Maria is settled down and living with her significant other. I see them occasionally at social events. They make for a happy, contented couple. I wish them continued happiness.

Angela is living alone and working at a career she dearly loves. Her divorce is final and her husband is giving her the financial security she needs to alleviate my ongoing concerns for her welfare.

Rosie is still my buddy. Our meetings never advanced beyond the congenial stage. The man she seeks is still out there, waiting, if she will stop looking.

Mamie is still my confidante. We were two old crabs locked into separate waters. She has resolved most of her problems with "the doctor", her significant other and life has become easier for her.

Mary and I were married. In the words of her pastor, a man needs a woman as a helpmate. In listening to his words of wisdom, I discovered in myself, or became assured myself, she is an ideal mate till death do us part. The marriage and life together holds much promise. I look forward to both in great expectation.

Postlude

The choice to remain single or remarry is a conscious one each widower makes for himself. Learning how to recognize what is best for your self is the purpose to which I have written this book. The events and incidences, peculiarities and similarities, I experienced have been for me an emotional trip to the Inn of my Second Happiness. I met six influential women in the transition from married, to widower, to married again. Each woman in her own way and by her own person and personality has helped bring me back from depths of depression and anxiety to the world of reality. As I related to another widower of some acquaintance, I know I can live alone, I also know I don't want to. I consider myself something of an unusual man in this respect. I enjoy the matrimonial state. Living alone has its advantages and if those advantages are what you seek then it is best to abide by them. For me they did not.

Another acquaintance remarked to me shortly after Betty died, "If you choose to marry again it must mean you had a good first marriage." In light of these past events I cannot disagree with either acquaintance. I did discover that by entering into a second marriage it would not pick up where the last marriage ended. The process of communicating and compromise begin again. I consider myself very lucky to have met Mary when I did. She brought me back to being myself again; the person I was before I met and married Betty; Not the person I was at the time of Betty's death. Should you, the reader choose to marry again, keep that singular thought in mind. Your new wife must compliment you in every way as your late wife, but she is not a substitute for her. She deserves to be recognized as her own person.

The Author's Reflections

I was the third born child to my father and mother. They divorced shortly after my birth. My own experience in dealing with divorce is it is a matter of choice and circumstance. From their experiences and others I have taken a position to not believe in divorce as a solution for a marriage that encounters difficulties. Hence, I would not enter into a marriage looking for an escape clause, which is what divorce has become. From what I learned of my parents and their subsequent divorce I concluded the only thing wrong with their marriage was they couldn't live under the same roof together. The love they held and still hold for one another is still there, it's no longer practiced as a couple. My mother later remarried and had two more children. That made me the middle child from my mother's womb. An ominous beginning since it seems my whole life has revolved around being in the middle. My father never remarried. He was content to remain single.

From the time the doctor informed me my wife could die quickly and unexpectedly I tried to prepare myself for that eventuality. It didn't work. At the precise moment of crisis my mind and body went completely numb and limp. Sudden death is not a moment that can be prepared for.

Even when the truth is known, the actual moment is a gut wrenching, horrible ordeal. Initially, after my wife died and the shock subsided after the funeral, I forced myself into a deep grieving state. My purpose was to get all those usurped feelings and emotions out of my system. The sooner the grief was gone the sooner I could return to living with myself, my family and my friends. I thought after four months I was done. I discovered over a year later I wasn't. The people around me who stated a year was necessary chagrined me. "Why a year?" I asked myself. "To what purpose?" I felt a year was a standard rule imposed in an outmoded form of etiquette. I had accepted my wife's passing and wanted to get back into living as soon as possible so all might return to being normal again before I had reason to believe this was all there was to living. Time and other relationships with other women proved to me how wrong I was. The healing takes much longer. I went out grasping at skirts, looking for a woman who closest suited my past life and would pick up where my previous relationship had ended. It doesn't work that way. As I began my emotional trip back to my adolescence I discovered a path taken is a path left behind. To begin a new journey a new starting point or an established starting point is necessary. I came back to the emotional age of 21 with the experienced age of 50 to begin my quest. It was from this point I met Mary who was also widowed. I have rediscovered through her a man does not love but once or only one way. He loves each woman differently and for different reasons. I have found in her more characteristics to my liking and another level of happiness. The same is true with her.

From this marriage we both made our vows a second time. And from those vows we repeated the words uttered so long ago - till death do us part.

Postscript II

"When the Lord Walked With Us"

A year has passed since our marriage. Mary being a religious woman has not only led me down the aisle of the church in marriage but has also brought me back into the church. At least every other week we attend services. I have observed and come to understand better, the religious aspects of renewed faith through my attendance. I have queried the religious outlooks of the church with her and have remembered the keener aspects of God's teachings. From within the sermons I have heard and in our private discussions later at home, I have connected more of the historical significance of religion with day-to-day living. It is from these sermons and discussions and some significant events of our marriage together, I have drawn a concluding thought.

The following concept of faith made a very significant impression upon us with regard to our future life together and amply postscripts our decision to marry.

"Footprints" is a short verse poem. I incorporate the literary work here for convenience and brevity.

"Footprints"

One night a man had a dream. He dreamed he was walking along the beach with the LORD. Across the sky flashed scenes from his life. For each scene, he noticed two sets of footprints in the sand, one belonging to him and the other to the LORD.

When the last scene of his life flashed before him, he looked back at the footprints in the sand. He noticed that many times along the path of his life there was only one set of footprints. He also noticed that it happened at the very lowest and saddest times in his life.

This really bothered him and he questioned the LORD about it. "LORD, you said that once I decided to follow you, You'd walk with me all the way. But I have noticed that during the most troublesome times in my life, there is but one set of footprints. I don't understand why when I needed you most, you should leave me."

The LORD replied, "My precious, precious child, I love you and I would never leave you. During your times of trial and suffering, when you see only one set of footprints, it was then I carried you."

In examining our lives before our marriage, no other event in either life was so traumatic and dramatic as to require the Lord's help to carry the burden for us as was the death of our spouses. I took the copy of "Footprints" I had and on it, I have added for Mary the dates of Sep 28, 1990 - Mar 9, 1996 and for me, Oct 17, 1992 - Mar 9, 1996, a time we feel, when the Lord surely walked with us. Amen.

Works Cited

Browning, Robert Hamilton. <u>Along the Road.</u>

Caine, Lynn. <u>Being a Widow.</u> New York: Arbor House William Morrow and Company, Inc., 1988.

Sexton, Robert. <u>Journeys of the Human Heart.</u> Colorado: Blue Mountain Arts, 1996.

Stevenson, Mary. <u>Footprints.</u>*

Sydnor, Rebecca. <u>Making Love Happen.</u> New York: British American Publishing, 1989.

* Mary Stevenson is the first of two authors to be granted copyright (1984) for this verse by the U.S. Copyright Office. Margaret Fishback Powers was the second author granted copyright (1987) for this verse by the U.S. Copyright Office. Slight variations exist between both versions in title and wording. It appears all over the world in derivative form under many names including Anonymous and Author Unknown.

Additional Recommended Reading

Barash, Susan Shapiro. <u>Second Wives: The Pitfalls and Rewards of Marrying Widowers and Divorced men.</u> New York: New Horizon Press, 2000.

Caine, Lynn. <u>Widow.</u> New York: Arbor House, 1988

Campbell, Scott and Silverman, Phyllis R. <u>Widower: When Men Are Left Alone.</u> New York: Baywood Publishing Company, 1996.

Levang, Elizabeth. <u>When Men Grieve: Why Men Grieve Differently and How You Can Help.</u> New York: Fairview Press, 1998.

Noel, Brooke and Blair, Pamela. <u>I Wasn't Ready To Say Goodbye: Surviving, Coping and healing After the Death of a Loved One.</u> New York: Champion Press LTD, 2000.

Wentworth, Theodore S. <u>Build a Better Spouse Trap: A Street Smart Strategy For Men Who Have Lost a Love.</u> New York: M. Evans and Company, 2002.